Secularism: A Very Short Introduction

Praise for the hardback: *Secularism: Politics, Religion, and Freedom*

'A timely tour de force and indispensable analysis for anyone seeking to get to grips with the roots, philosophy, and current controversies surrounding secularism which are challenging our vexed world.'

Professor Francesca Klug, author of *A Magna Carta For All Humanity: Homing in on Human Rights*

'Secularism is of growing importance all over the world, yet it is also an approach with deep roots reaching far back into our history. Andrew Copson elegantly explores this history as well as secularism's importance today, showing how it evolved and how it is the key to de-escalating so many of the modern world's points of conflict.'

Dan Snow, historian and broadcaster

'Andrew Copson is one of the most thoughtful people in the world on secularism. We have never needed a sane, intelligent, persuasive guide to secularism more than now—so I'd say thank God for this excellent book, if that wasn't too obviously ironic.'

Johann Hari

'This is an exceptionally careful, fair-minded and positive introduction to the many meanings of a word often carelessly used. It will be an enormous help to all who want to understand better the current controversies about religious belief and modern society.'

Rowan Williams

'A secular State embraces freedom of religion or belief, the equal treatment of persons regardless of faith, and the separation of religious and state authorities. In this wide-ranging and timely study Andrew Copson describes the virtues of secularism as the guarantor of equal dignity, freedom, and security for all, but also the various platforms from which it is opposed, and its fragile and increasingly beleaguered state across the world. Scrupulously fair, his book brings much-needed clarity into a confused and embittered area of dispute.'

Simon Blackburn, Fellow of Trinity College, Cambridge and Visiting Professor at the New College of the Humanities

'a concise and usefully nonpolemical summary of the wide variety of liberal secularisms around the world.'

Michael Ignatieff

'informative, admirably balanced, very well written, and full of examples…I cannot recommend this book too highly…This book prompts the reader to think deeply. Deservedly it will attract a wide audience both within and without the academy, not least as a first-rate teaching tool.'

Grace Davie, Professor Emeritus of Sociology at the University of Exeter and author of *Religion in Britain since 1945: Believing Without Belonging*

'A must read. It is a worthwhile introduction that will inform and may correct some assumptions and prejudices.'

The Rev Maurice Stafford, *Methodist Recorder*

'Concise and fair-minded…*Secularism* helps the reader navigate [the]…shifting terrain admirably.'

Nick Spencer, *Times Literary Supplement*

VERY SHORT INTRODUCTIONS are for anyone wanting a stimulating and accessible way into a new subject. They are written by experts, and have been translated into more than 45 different languages.

The series began in 1995, and now covers a wide variety of topics in every discipline. The VSI library currently contains over 600 volumes—a Very Short Introduction to everything from Psychology and Philosophy of Science to American History and Relativity—and continues to grow in every subject area.

Very Short Introductions available now:

Available soon:

For more information visit our website

www.oup.com/vsi/

Andrew Copson

SECULARISM

A Very Short Introduction

OXFORD
UNIVERSITY PRESS

OXFORD

UNIVERSITY PRESS

Great Clarendon Street, Oxford, OX2 6DP,
United Kingdom

Oxford University Press is a department of the University of Oxford.
It furthers the University's objective of excellence in research, scholarship,
and education by publishing worldwide. Oxford is a registered trade mark of
Oxford University Press in the UK and in certain other countries

First published in hardback as *Secularism: Politics,
Religion, and Freedom* 2017
First published as a Very Short Introduction 2019

Impression: 1

Published in the United States of America by Oxford University Press
198 Madison Avenue, New York, NY 10016, United States of America

British Library Cataloguing in Publication Data

Data available

Library of Congress Control Number: 2019936264

ISBN 978-0-19-874722-2

Printed in Great Britain by
Ashford Colour Press Ltd, Gosport, Hampshire

Contents

Foreword

Although secularism has been of fundamental importance in shaping the modern world, it is not as well-known a concept as capitalism or democracy or liberalism. As a political settlement it is not commonly studied in schools or even at universities. In these days, when all the implicit assumptions of liberal democracy are under strain, this is a dangerous situation.

Today we see too many glib attacks on the bogeyman of secularism by multiculturalists and religious fundamentalists. We also see the abuse of secularism by racists and xenophobes as a stick with which to beat minorities. Reasonable debates about secularism on the basis of a shared understanding of it, what it means, and where it came from, are in short supply. This book is not intended as an argument for secularism but as an introduction to it, in the hope that secularism will become better known as a concept and we can have more fruitful discussions and debates about it.

Religion and politics are notoriously two topics to avoid in polite company. The company I keep must not be polite, as long conversations with many friends and colleagues on both these topics have immeasurably improved this book. Needless to say, any errors or infelicities that remain are my own, but I would like to thank in particular Bob Churchill, Alex Jackson, David Pollock, and Richy Thompson. Thanks are also due to two anonymous

OUP readers, to Elizabeth O'Casey, who took out China, and to John Heyderman for the proof that Spinoza influenced Locke.

I would like to dedicate this book to Mark Wardrop, Julia Copson, and Maureen Cunningham, all of whom supported me while writing it in different ways.

List of illustrations

Chapter 1
What is secularism?

The British social reformer George Jacob Holyoake (1817–1906)
encouraged people to reject received wisdom and authoritarian
politics and instead to examine all claims in the light of reason
and science and with an eye to human progress. Inspired by a
previous generation of Enlightenment thinkers, he popularized
a this-worldly attitude to personal morals, to philosophy, and to
the organization of society and politics. He coined the word
'secularism' to describe his approach.

Today, the words 'atheist' (which he rejected as too negative)
or 'humanist' (not used by him but adopted by many of his
contemporaries and successors) do most of the job that Holyoake
meant 'secularist' to do, describing non-religious philosophies,
morals, and personal world views. The word 'secularism' still
has multiple meanings, but this book is about the most common
use of the word: an approach to the ordering of communities,
nations, and states.

We'll examine later the different definitions that exist even of
this specific political secularism, but a good provisional modern
definition is that adopted by the contemporary French scholar
of secularism Jean Baubérot. He sees secularism as made up of
three parts:

- separation of religious institutions from the institutions of the state and no domination of the political sphere by religious institutions;

- freedom of thought, conscience, and religion for all, with everyone free to change their beliefs and manifest their beliefs within the limits of public order and the rights of others;

- no state discrimination against anyone on grounds of their religion or non-religious world view, with everyone receiving equal treatment on these grounds.

This secularism is not fully implemented in any state and never has been, but is the ideal towards which secularists like Baubérot wish to move the political order.

Separation of religious institutions from state institutions

'Separation of church and state' first became a constitutional feature of some Western countries in the 18th century, but the separation of religious institutions from state ones had also been a feature of societies elsewhere and at other times in history. In the 20th century, many states in Asia and Africa also constitutionally declared this separation, following the Western models and their own traditions. Today, separation is seen by many as the modern and democratic ideal. In some states it is formal and official, expressed in constitutions and laws; in others it is not official but is a practical reality in the way that governments operate. Separation is not uncontroversial. It is opposed by those who think that the state should share their own religious identity and have that identity as its foundation. It is also opposed by those who think that making the state non-religious disadvantages religious people in some way and is unfair.

The background to the development of modern separation in Europe was a struggle for power between churches and governments. Far more commonly today, the avowed motive for separation is to give equality of citizenship to all people of all different beliefs and to avoid alienating them by declaring a state religion they don't share. Outside Europe many states still see religion and religious institutions as their rivals for power and for the loyalty of citizens. These states often regulate and control religious institutions as a result, and this too is a rejection of separation, or at least a denial that separation must entail non-interference.

Freedom of thought, conscience, and religion

This freedom has been a feature of a number of societies and legal regimes in history but was first elaborated as a legal right in the modern West. It evolved from the official policies of religious toleration that developed in the Netherlands and elsewhere in Europe as a way of recognizing an individual's conscience. It was in the guise of 'religious freedom' that it first became a legal right and under that name it is still a cherished part of US political culture in particular. Since the advent of formal universal human rights in the 1940s, it is now recognized as freedom of 'religion or belief', where the word 'belief' includes non-religious world views, and as being itself part of a wider freedom of thought and conscience.

According to the United Nations Human Rights Committee in 1993, the right to this freedom:

> is far-reaching and profound; it encompasses freedom of thought on all matters, personal conviction and the commitment to religion or belief, whether manifested individually or in community with others…protects theistic, non-theistic and atheistic beliefs, as well as the right not to profess any religion or belief…entails the freedom to choose a religion or belief, including the right to replace one's current religion or belief with another or to adopt atheistic views, as well as the right to retain one's religion or belief.

The Human Rights Committee also agrees with Baubérot's observation, however, that in some limited circumstances, it can be acceptable to restrict this freedom. They say that the right to have a religion or belief is protected 'unconditionally' and 'no one can be compelled to reveal his thoughts or adherence to a religion or belief' but that the right to act in accordance with your religion or belief may be subject to some limitations if they are 'prescribed by law and are necessary to protect public safety, order, health or morals, or the fundamental rights and freedoms of others'.

Equal treatment on grounds of religion or non-religious world view

Beyond simply protecting the freedom of people to hold and manifest their beliefs, the secular state envisaged by Baubérot goes further and guarantees equal treatment to all on grounds of their religion or non-religious world view. This idea was formalized more recently than the first two aspects of secularism. Internationally, it is set out in the 1981 *Declaration on the Elimination of All Forms of Intolerance and of Discrimination Based on Religion or Belief* by the United Nations General Assembly. This said, 'No one shall be subject to discrimination by any State, institution, group of persons, or person on grounds of religion or other beliefs.' The *Declaration* called on all states to 'take effective measures to prevent and eliminate discrimination on the grounds of religion or belief in the recognition, exercise and enjoyment of human rights and fundamental freedoms in all fields of civil, economic, political, social and cultural life'.

It's in Europe that the principle of equal treatment has been most extensively implemented in law and policy. Defining this approach as 'social equality of religion or belief', the political scientist Alan Carling analyses it as having three aspects:

- equal legal protection for individuals 'against unjust harms arising from their identities of religion or belief', which has been achieved by 'extending laws concerning discrimination, harassment, victimization or hate crime' to cover religion or belief;

- equal treatment for 'religions and belief systems themselves', meaning state authorities don't prefer one religion or belief over another in public life;

- equality of this principle of non-discrimination with other principles of non-discrimination. This means the state treats 'social identities of religion or belief on equal terms with other sources of social identity that are subject to legal regulation, such as gender, race, ethnicity, disability, age, sexuality and...social caste'.

We said that separation was originally a response by the state to the rival power of religion and that freedom of belief arose from a new recognition of the demands of conscience. Equal treatment arises out of a different and more modern challenge for states: that of managing relations between the citizens of their increasingly diverse societies in a way that keeps those societies peaceful and fair.

Although Holyoake coined the word secularism relatively recently and the three aspects identified by Baubérot have only in modern times been formalized, the idea of secularism is much older. It is true that, for much of history, there have been strong links between how human communities have organized themselves politically and the way they have organized their religious life. But this mixing up of religion and politics has not been universal, and even from the beginning of recorded history we can find the seeds of secularism being sown.

Chapter 2
Secularism in Western societies

Although they had public temples and their festivals were important civic occasions, in the city states of classical Greece gods and goddesses were not involved in 'politics' (literally in Greek 'the business of the city') in the sense of ordering the affairs of the human community. Aristotle (384BCE–322BCE), the first European to write a systematic analysis of politics, said the purpose of the city was 'the best and highest life possible'. The question of what was 'best and highest' was to be approached entirely in this-worldly terms, not in terms of the divine. The same attributes that were virtuous in a man, like justice, were to be judged virtuous in a city. As in much ancient Greek ethical thinking, the human world and the world of gods were quite distinct in moral terms.

This is a sort of secularism, in which the aims of the state are separate from religious aims, but it is not secularism in the full modern sense. Still, unlike in ancient Persia, where the Great King was not just a political leader but also the worldly agent of the one God, or in ancient Jewish society, where divine commandments had the force of law, many states in the ancient Greek world in the centuries after Aristotle offered an alternative model. This model of a just city, to be judged by human standards and with ends quite distinct from those of the divine, persisted as an idea in political thought. As the Roman Empire succeeded the multiple

6

city states of the Greek world, it inherited this intellectual tradition in combination with its own approach to religious beliefs and practices, which was often pragmatically pluralist.

Before conscious and deliberate separation of state and religion began in earnest, however, the multiple paganisms of the classical world gave way to an ideology that forced the two together as never before.

Christians and the idea of secularism

Christianity began in the Roman Empire with stories of a Jewish preacher whose followers after his death referred to him as Jesus Christ. They enlisted non-Jewish converts, took on some ideas of Greek philosophy and of other popular cults, and progressively grew into a significant social force. This growth was not without difficulties. The empire was religiously diverse: it contained people with beliefs in many different gods and goddesses, as well as those who believed in none. But everyone within the empire was required on request to conform to the worship of the gods and of deified emperors. This involved paying at least lip service to them with oaths when called on to do so in the course of public life. Christians, like Jews, believed in only one god and were unwilling to acknowledge any others. For the first two centuries or so of their existence they risked social exclusion and official harassment as a result of their nonconformity.

In spite of (perhaps because of) their unusual beliefs and their occasional persecution, Christians continued to win converts and their social influence continued to grow. In 313, when they could no longer be marginalized, they were granted freedom of religion by Emperors Licinius (*c*.263–325) and Constantine (*c*.272–337). In 325 Constantine, who at some point became a Christian himself, convened a meeting of Christian leaders at Nicaea in present-day Turkey to settle vexed theological disputes. They produced the systematized doctrine known as the Nicene Creed and, in the decades that followed, the policy of the imperial state was one of tolerance for Christianity alongside its traditional cults. In 380, Christians went from being tolerated to being dominant when Emperor Theodosius (347–395) issued the Edict of Thessalonica, making it compulsory within Roman lands to be a Christian (specifically a Christian who accepted the Nicene Creed: all others were officially castigated as 'heretics'). In under a century, in one of the swiftest changes of fortunes in history, Christianity had gone from being a despised minority sect to the state religion of a continental empire.

Official persecution at the hands of a state entwined with a competing theology, toleration in a political order more at ease with religious diversity, and finally state authority as official cult of the era's superpower: the political standing of early Christians changed bewilderingly fast. Christian thought in relation to politics and church–state relations as it proceeded to work itself out over the centuries was to be similarly complex. Christianity created new concepts of heresy and orthodoxy, which would resound down the centuries. Pivotally for the history of secularism, it also contained at least the seed of a distinction between the church on the one hand and the state on the other, partly as a result of its Greek heritage, partly from its own developing theological resources, partly from its historical conditions.

To be sure, this seed took a while to germinate. The early trend in Christianity was to enlist the state in the service of religion just as the state had previously served the cults of emperors and the traditional Olympian gods. One prominent Christian leader named Ambrose (c.340–397) was typical in this. He successfully convinced Theodosius to persecute pagans and not to punish some Christians who destroyed a synagogue, saying it was after all 'a home of unbelief...which God Himself has condemned'. This usurpation of the rule of law on grounds of Christian exceptionalism was commonplace. Bishops down the centuries urged governments of every sort towards the promotion of

Christianity, persecution of non-Christians, and enforcement of the ethics of Christianity through the legal system.

In spite of all this, the demarcation of the worldly and the religious was an explicit possibility in Christian thought in a way it had never been when state and religion were married in the person of the emperor as political leader, high priest, and something close to a god. Right at the start of Christian academic thinking, the bishop Augustine (354–430) distinguished in his writings between the 'City of God' and the city in the regular world of states, laws, and earthly powers.

Nearly a millennium later Thomas Aquinas (1225–74) penned the first substantial Christian contribution to the question of church–state relations. In his writings he distinguished between law made by human beings (*lex humana*) and law made by God transmitted to human beings through revelation (*lex divina*). He was influenced by Aristotle, whose ideas, as we saw, carried the implication of secularism. But in no way did Aquinas agree with Aristotle that human beings make the *lex humana* according to their own needs. For him, the *lex humana* was a mere reflection of the divinely ordained laws of nature and good only to the extent that it accurately reflected those laws. It could always be overruled by the *lex divina*, to which it was inferior. Aquinas also asserted that, although monarchs were God's appointed representatives in their territories, the church was above them in relation to ethics. This may all seem unlikely to contribute to an idea of secularism. Nonetheless, his writings delineated the roles of the temporal and religious powers and Aquinas saw the monarch and the church as separate, even if he did not see them as equal.

Between the end of the ancient world and the beginning of the early modern world, organized Christianity was a political force as well as a religion. Throughout this period there was continual tension between the 'temporal' power in the form of monarchs and oligarchies, and those more directly dedicated to Jesus and

God in the form of priests, bishops, and popes. Aquinas's thought was an academic reflection of this tension. In the real world of politics it showed itself as a struggle for power between competing visions of government.

Representative of one end of the spectrum was a decree known as *Unam sanctam* issued in 1302 by Pope Boniface VIII (*c.*1230–1303). Boniface declared that there was no salvation for any human being outside the Catholic Church and that the Pope's position as head of the Catholic Church entitled him to the loyalty of everyone. In particular all monarchs and magistrates must submit to papal authority. This was not popular with monarchs. The king of France, who had been a particular target of the decree, gave a practical rebuttal of it by having the Pope charged, arrested, and briefly imprisoned.

At the other end of the spectrum from *Unam sanctam* was a law passed in England in 1534 under King Henry VIII (1491–1547). The *Act of Supremacy* declared the monarch to be the 'the only supreme head on Earth of the Church of England'. In 1539 the *Act Abolishing Diversity in Opinions* reiterated the fact that the king was the head of the church—'in God's law, supreme head immediately under Him of this whole church and congregation of England'—and demanded conformity in religious opinions of every English person. Any who did not conform were to suffer legal penalties, up to and including death. Religion was to be mandated by the monarch, who, while still seeing himself and the state as Catholic, had usurped the traditional role of the church.

In the 16th century, the church in Western Europe split into the Roman Catholic Church, on the one hand, and a variety of denominations, loosely termed as 'Protestant', on the other. This 'Reformation' was begun in 1517 by the German priest Martin Luther (1483–1546), who protested at what he saw as theological errors in the doctrine of the Roman Catholic Church. As part of his project of challenging the church, he made a serious theoretical contribution to resolving the centuries-old ambiguity of church–state relations within Christianity.

Luther preached a sermon in which he spoke of two kinds of righteousness. One was righteousness 'in the eyes of God' (*coram deo*); the second was righteousness 'in the eyes of the world' (*coram mundo*). Righteousness *coram mundo* was exhibited not only by Christians but by adherents of other creeds and, although no guarantee of salvation if not accompanied by righteousness *coram deo*, it was praiseworthy in its own limited right. Obeying the law, paying your taxes, and helping your friends, neighbours, and fellow citizens: this civil righteousness had value. Luther's idea of these two realms laid the foundations for a political belief that princes should not interfere in or coerce faith and that government's right to prescribe behaviours should not trespass on the territory of religion but was limited to the civil realm.

Three centuries later, the American secularist James Madison said that Luther 'led the way' in delineating church and state. In fact the Reformation sparked more than a century of religious warfare which ended with a system in Europe that brought church and state closer together, though with the advantage now firmly with the state. The principle of '*cuius regio, eius religio*' ('Whose realm, his religion'), first formulated in the Treaty of Augsburg in 1555, held that the religion of the state was to be determined by its ruler. When the Peace of Westphalia mostly ended the European wars of religion in 1648, all parties agreed this pragmatic compromise. If a monarch were a Roman Catholic, Lutheran, or Calvinist, then that would be the religion of his or her realm, but those living within the realm who adhered to either of the other denominations were to have the right to practise their religion freely in private or to leave the realm for one of their own religion.

Christians who suffered under government of a different denomination reacted to this theologically. The denomination that became known as Baptists moved furthest in elaborating a theology of secularism as a result. Founded by John Smyth and Thomas Helwys at the beginning of the 17th century, this denomination was formed of English people who had fled to Holland to escape Anglican persecution (it was a Baptist—Edward Wightman—who in 1611 became the last heretic to be executed by burning in England). One of their foundational beliefs was that baptism into Christianity was suitable only for those who had reached their faith by the exercise of their own reason. Because of this and the persecution they themselves had faced, Baptists developed the separation of church and state as a fundamental principle. Roger Williams (c.1603–83) tried to put this principle into practice in a colony he founded in North America. Settled in 1636, Providence—in present-day Rhode Island—was to be a place of absolute freedom of religion for all, Christian and non-Christian (as Williams later wrote, 'paganish, Jewish, Turkish or anti-Christian consciences and worships') alike. In 1644, Williams published *The Bloody Tenet of Persecution, for Cause of Conscience*, arguing that Christianity demanded that civil power must not enforce any religion. Williams's colony was not a success, but his writing is a good example of how far Christianity could go at that time in advocating separation of church and state and freedom of religion.

Enlightenment and the theory of secularism

The ideas and arguments of the Baptists combined with academic philosophy to influence the English thinker John Locke (1632–1704), who took the idea of state and church separation onto new theoretical ground. In *On The Difference Between Civil and Ecclesiastical Power* (1674), he distinguished between two aspects of society which he claimed were discernible almost everywhere. The first was 'Civil Society, or the State'; the second was 'Religious Society, or the Church'. The purpose of the church was to 'attain happiness after this life in another world' whereas the purpose of the state was:

civil peace and prosperity...the preservation of the society and
every member thereof in a free and peaceable enjoyment of all the
good things that belong to each of them.

Concerned with worldly matters alone, the state had no justification
for meddling with anything 'beyond the concernments of this life'
and whereas the state could use violence to enforce its laws, the
church could not. The church's inducements to obey its laws were
the promise of happiness or threat of punishment after death.

In *A Letter Concerning Toleration* (1689), Locke addressed further
the question of how government should deal with competing
religions among citizens. He argued that, on the basis of the
distinction between state and church he had elaborated, there was
no reason for the state to persecute those who had Protestant
beliefs that differed from those of the state church. In fact, he said,
persecution itself caused civil unrest inimical to the ends the state
was bound to secure. Roman Catholics and atheists ought not to
be tolerated, but this was for secular, not religious, reasons: the
former owed allegiance to the Pope, a foreign prince, and the
latter didn't believe in any transcendent source of morality that
could guarantee their oath and so couldn't be trusted.

Locke saw religion as a private matter in that a person's religious
views and the truth of them (and hence whether that person will
attain happiness after death or not) do not affect any other person.
He had lived for a time in the Netherlands and experienced its
tolerant approach and was also influenced by the Dutch philosopher
Baruch Spinoza (1632–77), who wrote in favour of the state being
a bulwark against religious oppression. The approach of these two
philosophers, far more interested in state than church, coloured
intellectual consideration of religion and government in the
decades that followed. This theorizing was enabled and encouraged
by the increasing power of the state, which by now had grown in
influence and wealth relative to the church. Decreasingly reliant
on churches for education and social welfare, the state also had

less need of the church for legitimacy or the keeping of social order. It is at this point that the question of church and state in Europe tilts away from Christianity and towards the way of thinking known as 'Enlightenment'.

The age of Enlightenment in European thought runs from the late 17th to the late 18th century and is characterized by the growth of science and by the challenging of dogma and pursuit of freedom in academic, political, and personal life. The thinkers seen as part of this movement had diverse ideas, but their work on church and state gave birth to a full theory of secularism that for the first time affected the policy of states in the real world. Crucially, all important Enlightenment thinkers derived the legitimacy of government not from God or the approval of churches, but from the consent of the governed.

The philosophers of the Enlightenment did not seek consensus. They embraced a bubbling intellectual ferment and were always disputing with each other. Still, they all agreed that the yoking of state to church was spurious. The Christian lawyer and philosopher Montesquieu (1689–1755) wrote in *The Spirit of the Laws* (1748) that, although they may exert moral influence on bad laws and governments, religions ought not to involve the state in their own religious disputes. He observed the division between church and state propounded by Locke and asserted that religions should not be taken as the foundation of the state. Non-Christians like Voltaire (1694–1778), David Hume (1711–76), and Adam Smith (1723–90) agreed, and all endorsed the freedom of religion that Locke and Spinoza had advocated.

Jean-Jacques Rousseau (1712–78), although he would have allowed his ideal state to enforce considerable cultural homogeneity, argued in *Of the Social Contract* (1762) that no just state could deny religious toleration. Divorcing the aims of the state from the aims of the church, the philosopher Denis Diderot (1713–84) published in his *Encyclopaedia* that 'the good of the people must be the great purpose of government…And the greatest good of the people is liberty. It is to the state what health is to the individual.' More assertively anti-church, Baron d'Holbach (1723–89) condemned its official status in *Christianity Unveiled* (1767) saying

> it is as a citizen that I attack it, because it seems to me harmful to the happiness of the state, hostile to the march of the mind of man, and contrary to sound morality, from which the interests of state policy can never be separated.

In 1777 a *Statute of Religious Freedom* was drafted in the state of Virginia in North America which could trace its descent all the way back through the intellectual stages that we have examined. It was made law in 1786 and the blending of Protestant Christian political theology and the humanist political theory of the Enlightenment in its ideas and its language is obvious.

Box 1 An act for establishing religious freedom

Whereas, Almighty God hath created the mind free;

That all attempts to influence it by temporal punishments or burthens, or by civil incapacitations tend only to beget habits of hypocrisy and meanness, and therefore are a departure from the plan of the holy author of our religion, who being Lord, both of body and mind yet chose not to propagate it by coercions on either, as was in his Almighty power to do,

That the impious presumption of legislators and rulers, civil as well as ecclesiastical, who, being themselves but fallible and uninspired men have assumed dominion over the faith of others, setting up their own opinions and modes of thinking as the only true and infallible, and as such endeavouring to impose them on others, hath established and maintained false religions over the greatest part of the world and through all time;

(*continued*)

Box 1 Continued

That to compel a man to furnish contributions of money for the propagation of opinions, which he disbelieves is sinful and tyrannical;

That even the forcing him to support this or that teacher of his own religious persuasion is depriving him of the comfortable liberty of giving his contributions to the particular pastor, whose morals he would make his pattern, and whose powers he feels most persuasive to righteousness, and is withdrawing from the Ministry those temporary rewards, which, proceeding from an approbation of their personal conduct are an additional incitement to earnest and unremitting labours for the instruction of mankind;

That our civil rights have no dependence on our religious opinions any more than our opinions in physics or geometry,

That therefore the proscribing any citizen as unworthy the public confidence, by laying upon him an incapacity of being called to offices of trust and emolument, unless he profess or renounce this or that religious opinion, is depriving him injuriously of those privileges and advantages, to which, in common with his fellow citizens, he has a natural right,

That it tends only to corrupt the principles of that very Religion it is meant to encourage, by bribing with a monopoly of worldly honours and emoluments those who will externally profess and conform to it;

That though indeed, these are criminal who do not withstand such temptation, yet neither are those innocent who lay the bait in their way;

That to suffer the civil magistrate to intrude his powers into the field of opinion and to restrain the profession or propagation of principles on supposition of their ill tendency is a dangerous fallacy which at once destroys all religious liberty because he being of course judge of that tendency will make his opinions the rule of judgment and approve or condemn the sentiments of others only as they shall square with or differ from his own;

That it is time enough for the rightful purposes of civil government, for its officers to interfere when principles break out into overt acts against peace and good order;

And finally, that Truth is great, and will prevail if left to herself, that she is the proper and sufficient antagonist to error, and has nothing to fear from the conflict, unless by human interposition disarmed of her natural weapons free argument and debate, errors ceasing to be dangerous when it is permitted freely to contradict them:

Be it enacted by General Assembly that no man shall be compelled to frequent or support any religious worship, place, or ministry whatsoever, nor shall be enforced, restrained, molested, or burthened in his body or goods, nor shall otherwise suffer on account of his religious opinions or belief, but that all men shall be free to profess, and by argument to maintain, their opinions in matters of Religion, and that the same shall in no wise diminish, enlarge or affect their civil capacities. And though we well know that this Assembly elected by the people for the ordinary purposes of Legislation only, have no power to restrain the acts of succeeding Assemblies constituted with powers equal to our own, and that therefore to declare this act irrevocable would be of no effect in law; yet we are free to declare, and do declare that the rights hereby asserted, are of the natural rights of mankind, and that if any act shall be hereafter passed to repeal the present or to narrow its operation, such act will be an infringement of natural right.

The principal shift between the Christian way of thinking and the Enlightenment way of thinking came in the idea that the people had to consent to their government for it to be legitimate. It was revolutionaries in two countries who made this idea a reality and, in doing so, established official state secularism for the first time.

France and *laïcité*

Although it was the homeland of many Enlightenment philosophers, France in the 18th century was a nation in which the monarch still exercised authoritarian political power. That power was intertwined with dogmatic and influential Roman Catholic institutions in the social and political system that was later called the *ancien régime*. When the French Revolution erupted in 1789 to sweep that old system away, both Crown and church were equal targets. New laws had to be drafted, and an elected assembly produced the *Déclaration des droits de l'homme et du citoyen* (*Declaration of Human and Civic Rights*). Its principles drew heavily on Enlightenment thinking, and freedom of thought and religion were declared among the rights:

> No one may be disturbed on account of his opinions, even religious ones, as long as the manifestation of such opinions does not interfere with the established Law and Order. (Article 10 of the *Déclaration des droits de l'homme et du citoyen*)

This declaration was accompanied by the dismantling of the state power of the church and seizure of its assets. The church was the largest landowner in pre-revolutionary France; now its property was confiscated by the state. Clergy, who had wielded power as the 'First Estate' (most important class) under the *ancien régime*, were stripped of their special rights, made public employees, and required to take an oath of loyalty to the state.

The French Revolution was not a single event but a decade-long series of innovations from 1789 to 1799 at the end of which a coup brought Napoleon into power, first as a consul in a triumvirate and then as Emperor of the French. In that decade the link between the French state and the Catholic Church was comprehensively broken, and France experienced what some historians call the attempted 'de-Christianization' of its society and politics. Christian moral assumptions were removed from the laws of the state, as with the legalization of divorce in 1792. New public bodies took on institutional functions that had been fulfilled by the church, such as the registration of births, marriages, and deaths.

The campaign of de-Christianization included some aspects that now seem very odd. Rousseau had thought that a republic, deprived of traditional religiosity to bind together its citizens, needed mystical aspects that would inspire emotion. Inspired by him, ultra-revolutionaries such as Jacques Hébert (1757–94) advocated new festivals and holidays for France, and even a new non-theistic state religion—the Cult of Reason—for which a lavish festival was organized in 1793 by the scientist Pierre Gaspard Chaumette (1763–94). It was held in the cathedral of Notre-Dame, where the Christian altar was replaced by one to Liberty, with women dressed up as sexually provocative 'Goddesses of Reason'. In 1794, the idea of an atheistic state cult was officially rejected, when the National Convention under revolutionary leader Robespierre (1758–94) adopted a deistic national religion of 'the Supreme Being'. Its first festival was held on an artificial mountain in Paris and celebrated nationwide on a massive scale, but this cult too was short-lived, barely surviving Robespierre himself when he died by guillotine the same year.

As the fight for freedom tipped over into the persecution of past oppressors, public Christian worship was banned or strictly limited. Having invaded the Papal States in Italy and declared a Roman Republic, the French revolutionary government even imprisoned the reigning Pope, Pius VI. He died in prison in France in 1799. There was violence against Christians and their clergy throughout the period of the revolution. Priests were subject to official harassment, deportation, and execution; many fled France. Mob and state violence rose in the mid-1790s to fever pitch and can justly be called a persecution of Christians. Certainly, it did not live up to the freedom of conscience for all citizens declared in 1789.

In the late 1790s, the radical period of de-Christianization began to abate and Napoleon put an end to it. In 1801 he negotiated a treaty with Pope Pius VII, representing the Roman Catholic Church. This so-called *Concordat* was ratified by the French state in 1802, with extra provisions added unilaterally by Napoleon. As a result of these measures, the Roman Catholic Church was again recognized as 'the religion of the majority of the French', but there was no restoration of its power to pre-revolutionary heights. The land and assets confiscated in the revolution were gone forever and although priests were allowed to return and restore the religious life of their parishes to some extent, mayors could prohibit worship if they found it disturbed public peace, and a raft of police regulations applied. Crucially, there was no question of restoring the confessional uniformity of society that had been the state's aim under the monarchy. State recognition and funding were extended not just to Roman Catholicism but also to the Protestant denominations of Calvinism and Lutheranism and, in a move opposed by many Christians, to Judaism. Jews were emancipated throughout French territories in Europe, relieved of the civil and political disabilities that had been placed on them under Christian states, given freedom to worship, and released from ghettos. In addition to this confessional pluralism, the French state instituted its own control over large parts of church life: selecting bishops, salarying priests, and regulating the seminaries where they were trained. The recognized Protestant churches were also regulated, and a government department was established to oversee all these religious matters.

The settlement of 1802 proved no final answer as to what should be the relationship between church and state in France.

Throughout the 19th century there was a struggle for power and influence between the secularist (generally leftist and republican) and clerical (generally conservative and sometimes monarchical) tendencies in French political and social life. In the course of this struggle the French word *laïcité* was coined. Like the English word secularism, *laïcité* had and still has many meanings, but the principal one was to describe the separation of church and state along the lines that French history indicated—a republican ethic that would rid civil life of religious interference and guarantee freedom of conscience to all people in their common aspect as citizens.

The idea of *laïcité* gained ground until, in the phase of French constitutional history known as the Third Republic (1870–1940), it came to be a defining ideology of the state. This secularizing period culminated with the passing of a law 'on the separation of Churches and the State' in 1905 (see Figure 1) but began with Republican dominance of the government from 1879 onwards. Compulsory prayers at the opening of Parliament, chaplains in the military, Catholic symbols on public buildings and monuments—all were abolished. State-funded health and education services were secularized. Clergy were removed from the boards of hospitals and the faculties of schools. A new national education system with no religious instruction was introduced for all children.

As the culmination of these reforms, the 1905 law declared: 'The Republic ensures freedom of conscience. It guarantees the free exercise of religion under the provisos enacted hereafter in the interest of public order.' It abolished the state recognition and funding of selected religions that had been established by Napoleon, abrogated the *Concordat* of 1801, and removed the national official status of the Catholic Church. (It also offered confiscated church property back to religious organizations, but the Roman Catholic Church declined the offer, leaving the state to this day to own and maintain all their pre-1905 churches for them.)

1. French allegorical picture postcard from 1905 showing the
separation of Church and State, with the latter a more appealing figure.

The 1905 law has more or less endured. It was embedded into the constitution of the current (Fifth) French Republic on its formation in 1958, as was the 1789 *Déclaration* with its own insistence on freedom of thought. As a result of these provisions, France can claim to be secular in that there is no domination of state institutions by religious organizations, and the law provides for freedom of religion or belief. Recent controversy over the treatment of Muslims in particular has, however, called into question its commitment to the equality of persons of all beliefs, as we shall see later.

America and freedom of religion

France was not the first nation in the 18th century to declare new liberties and in doing so make new pronouncements about the relationship between religion and the state. The American Revolution, in which the colonists of the eastern coast of North America declared independence from Great Britain, predated the French. But in relation to secularism, this revolution took quite a different course.

In the *Declaration of Independence* that was signed and promulgated by the British Americans in 1776, they avowed that 'all men are created equal...endowed by their Creator with certain unalienable Rights'. This invocation of a deity, albeit a non-denominational one, contrasts with the French materialist assertion that 'all men are born free'. The contrast should not be overdone—other revolutionary documents such as the Virginian *Declaration of Rights* and the Massachusetts *Constitution* describe men as 'by nature equally free and independent' and 'born free and equal', and the *Declaration of Independence* was never given constitutional significance. But in the American Revolution that followed, there was certainly no anticlerical element and none of the general hostility towards religion that coloured the French experience.

In 1788 a permanent federal constitution was agreed by all the states of the new republic. In Section 3 of Article 6, this constitution stated that 'no religious test shall ever be required as a qualification to any office or public trust under the United States'. This contrasted with the situation then prevailing in England, where public office was confined to members of the Church of England, and established in the new state one of the essential aspects of secularism: non-discrimination in matters of religion or belief.

The constitution was widely criticized for omitting the protection of a number of rights seen as fundamental and so was amended in 1791. The ten amendments were known as *The Bill of Rights*, and the first of them, known ever since as *The First Amendment*, stated that the legislature, among other things could 'make no law respecting an establishment of religion, or prohibiting the free exercise thereof'. These two short clauses became known as the 'establishment clause' and 'free exercise clause' respectively. They introduced two further aspects of secularism to the US: the separation of state institutions from religious ones and freedom of religion. Thomas Jefferson (1743–1826), a prominent revolutionary who went on to be president (1801–9), highlighted the importance of these principles when writing to Baptists in Connecticut a decade later:

> Believing with you that religion is a matter which lies solely between man and his God, that he owes account to none other for his faith or his worship, that the legislative powers of government reach actions only, and not opinions, I contemplate with sovereign reverence that act of the whole American people which declared that their legislature would 'make no law respecting an establishment of religion, or prohibiting the free exercise thereof', thus building a wall of separation between Church and State.

Jefferson had drafted the *Statute for Religious Freedom* for the state of Virginia in 1777 (see Figure 2), but US law now went

2. Thomas Jefferson was so proud of his contribution to secularist law that he had it inscribed on his gravestone.

beyond that in declaring not just religious freedom but an explicitly non-religious basis for the state. In 1797 the United States ratified a treaty with the Islamic government in Tripoli that declared 'the Government of the United States of America is not, in any sense, founded on the Christian Religion'.

James Madison (1751–1836), Jefferson's immediate successor as president (1809–17), was his equal in devout adherence to separation on grounds of freedom, and by 1833 all the individual states of the US had followed the federal state in ending their church establishments. The secular settlement seemed secure. But in fact it experienced considerable anti-secularist backlash from the mid-19th century as Christians who had always seen the US as a Christian nation sought to have this reflected in the law. From the 1860s, under the banner of the National Reform Association, they lobbied for the inclusion of Christianity in the Constitution. They claimed that this would not be establishment, as no particular denomination was to be made the state's preferred church: just Christianity in general. The Association was unsuccessful and wound up in the 1940s, but proposals for its 'Christian Amendment' were discussed by Congress a number of times before then. Similar proposals sponsored by evangelical Protestants were brought throughout the 20th century with similar lack of success, but campaigns in the 19th and 20th centuries to add 'In God We Trust' to coins and paper currency and in 1954 the phrase 'under God' to the Pledge of Allegiance were successful.

Countervailing secularist attempts to strengthen constitutional secularism (now using this word) were completely unsuccessful. Partly in reaction to the activities of the National Reform Association, a number of religious and non-religious groups and individuals formed the National Liberal League to combat what they saw as attempts to violate the First Amendment. From the 1870s they promoted instead an expansion of the First Amendment to remove ambiguities and prevent 'in any degree a union of Church and State, or granting any special privilege, immunity or advantage to any sect or religious body, or to any number of sects or religious bodies'. Practices such as tax exemptions for churches, religiously inspired laws—such as the protection of the Sabbath—and prayers in state schools were all highlighted as violations.

The political failure of secularists owed much to the nature of American society, which was strongly Christian, and Protestant in particular. Christians had greeted the election of a non-Christian like Jefferson with dismay and it wasn't until the mid-20th century that a Roman Catholic was elected president. A smear of godlessness was enough to stymie the electoral hopes of many candidates for elected office at any level, especially in the 20th century, when not being religious was associated with Communism and hence antipathy to America itself. As a result, whereas secularism in France proceeded in fits and starts through a constitutionally tumultuous century, the elaboration of secularism in the US proceeded through the courts. Their interpretation of the establishment and free exercise clauses has defined the nature of American secularism.

The establishment clause on the face of it prohibits only one thing: the preferring of one religion above others. The Supreme Court, however, has interpreted it as meaning that to be constitutional a law must (i) have a secular purpose, not a religious one, (ii) not have the primary effect of advancing or inhibiting religious practice, and (iii) not give rise to 'excessive entanglement' of government and religion. The third limb of this test emerged in 1971, when the Supreme Court ruled against the state funding of Catholic schools, but throughout the 1960s the Court had already ruled against prayers and Bible readings in schools on the basis of the first two principles alone. In the 1990s the Court elaborated a test of 'coercion' as a way of determining whether the establishment clause was engaged, ruling unconstitutional anything that tended to force people into religious practice against their will.

One of the main question for judges in applying the free exercise clause has been whether citizens professing a religious motivation for acting in a certain way can rely on the clause to justify their actions, even if their actions break a law that applies to everybody else. Mormons in the late 19th century argued that they should be allowed bigamy because it was part of their religion, even though there was a general law against it. The Supreme Court ruled against them, finding that although the clause protected beliefs, it did not extend to allowing all actions that might arise from those beliefs. A general law that incidentally infringed an individual's religious freedom was not unconstitutional. In the 1960s, the Court changed tack. Ruling in favour of the unemployment benefit claim of a Seventh Day Adventist, whose religion mandated Saturday as a day of rest and who could not find work as a result, it now said that states wishing to apply laws that would even indirectly prevent free exercise needed to demonstrate a 'compelling interest' for doing so. In the 1990s the pendulum swung back and the Court reintroduced a distinction between beliefs and actions, ruling against two Native Americans who had taken drugs for religious purposes and lost their jobs as a result. Laws not intentionally directed at limiting free exercise but which did so only indirectly could now be upheld if the government had a 'rational basis' for the laws. Concern over this prompted Congress to pass the Religious Freedom Restoration Act in 1993, which attempted to reintroduce the 'compelling interest' test, which has since been upheld by the Court at least at the federal level.

The Court has taken a meandering path in its application of the free exercise clause. At every stage, its judgements have been controversial and unpredictable, but always they have sought to provide freedom of religion as far as is possible.

The fledgling United States of America, unlike pre-revolutionary France, had no single Christian denomination against whose repressive dominance it needed to assert itself. The US was a denominationally diverse society, and many of the colonists whose descendants declared independence had first left Europe as members of churches persecuted in the Old World. Because of this and of its later history, US secularism is expressed more as a guarantee of freedom of religion than as a civic identity to replace religious affiliation. Separation of church and state is simply the mechanism by which that freedom is secured. Even today, most Americans, unlike most French, feel no attachment to 'secularism'—it is 'religious freedom' that they value. Nonetheless and by whatever name, the US ranks relatively highly on all three aspects of secularism. In consequence of the establishment clause there is no mixing up of state and religious institutions; because of the free exercise clause there is as much freedom of conscience for individuals as is compatible with the rights of others; and there is a high level of equal treatment. It is not only those on the left and liberals who support this: even the conservative President Reagan declared proudly:

> We establish no religion in this country, we command no worship, we mandate no belief, nor will we ever. Church and state are, and must remain, separate. All are free to believe or not believe, all are free to practice a faith or not, and those who believe are free, and should be free, to speak of and act on their belief.

Modern Western societies

In the early years of the 21st century there are various religion–state configurations in what we broadly term 'the West' (Europe, the Americas, Oceania) but everywhere there is a distance between religious institutions and state institutions that would have been unthinkable in the days of Christendom. Not religion, but the rule of law through non-religious values embedded in constitutions has become the foundation of most states. Even where secularism is not official, a secular ethic has emerged in practice as many political values and civil and criminal laws have changed their foundation from a shared religion to a non-religious basis. Beyond that, there is great diversity of arrangements in constitutions and laws, mainly adopted in the 19th and 20th centuries. These state arrangements are products of the national history and culture of the individual societies and are seldom unambiguously secular. We will come later to consider some of these arrangements but for now, we turn from Western societies to those of a continent just as important for understanding secularism, and where it has both long roots and present-day significance.

Chapter 3
Secularism diversifies

Explicit secularism as a constitutional principle arose in Europe and saw its first formal establishment in the constitutions of European states and their settler colonies. In Asia in the 19th and 20th centuries, many reformers saw this secularism as an exemplar for their new political orders. Many Asian states went on to adopt a form they called secular, but in practice this conceals a diversity of ways of organizing religion. Nor are these forms solely the result of European influence; many parts of Asia had resources within their own political and religious traditions with which to form their secularism. Examination of just two avowedly secular states demonstrates this.

Turkey: the *laik* republic

The specific flavours of French and American secularism were products of their religious and political history. In Turkey, the first majority-Muslim society to declare its government secular, the same was true. From 1299 to the 19th century, Turkey was a powerful empire. At the head of this 'Ottoman Empire' was the *Sultan*, and he was not just a political leader: he was also a religious one. From the beginning, the sultans had claimed to be *caliphs*: spiritual and temporal leaders of all Muslims divinely selected to inherit the authority of Mohammed, the founder of

Islam. The Ottoman Empire was declared by its rulers to be a *caliphate*—an Islamic state ruled by religious law handed down by God.

The empire was a formidable power for many centuries. Its conquest of Constantinople in 1453 brought the Christian eastern Roman Empire to an end, and at its height the caliphate covered most of North Africa and the Arab world. It conquered large parts of Europe, including the Balkans and Greece, pushing almost to Vienna. By the 19th century, however, it was being squeezed by the industrialized European powers, which were outperforming it economically and militarily. In response the empire embarked on a period of reform called the *Tanzimât* ('Reorganization') to secure itself against competition from European states as well as the increasing nationalism of its European (and mainly Christian) subject peoples.

The reforms began in 1839 with the Edict of Gülhane, which included a declaration of equality before the law for all imperial subjects, Muslim or not. Power was re-centralized and attempts were made to give a sense of shared Ottoman citizenship to the empire's diverse nations. Because it was influenced by reforms in France, this process brought a secularization of many laws that had previously been based on Islamic principles. Homosexuality was decriminalized, slavery was abolished, proclamations were made in favour of freedom of religion for Christians and Jews, secular courts were introduced alongside the courts that applied Islamic law (sharia), and some state schools were opened with a secular curriculum. The reformers were self-consciously emulating the European powers and coupled the legal changes with mimicry of their culture. Government officials were encouraged to wear more Western clothing and adopt other Western habits. In spite of all this, the Ottoman Empire remained a caliphate. The constitution adopted in 1876 stated that the duty of the legislature was to implement the principles of the sharia and that the religion of the state was Islam. And although some secularization had been introduced, it was not by popular demand or revolution but by order of the Sultan and Caliph.

Far from containing nationalist and Christian demands, the *Tanzimât* stimulated them further. The empire lost territories throughout the late 19th and early 20th century, including all its majority-Christian European lands. Allying with Germany in the First World War, it also lost much of its non-European lands to Germany's victorious enemies. Years of political turmoil led in 1922 to revolution, the abolition of the empire, and the establishment of a republic in Turkey in 1923.

The principal leader of this revolution was Mustafa Kemal (1881–1938). Now considered the founder of modern Turkey, he took the honorific name *Atatürk* in 1934 and it is as Atatürk he is now known. Army officer turned revolutionary turned statesman, Atatürk was the leader of the Republican People's Party and president of Turkey from 1923 until his death. He was also the foremost secularist of the early republic. When the first republican constitution was adopted in 1924, it declared the religion of the state to be Islam but this provision was removed in 1928, and in 1937 it was stated in the constitution that the republic was *laik* ('secular'). In the intense revolutionary years between 1924 and his death, none of the religious elements of the Ottoman state was left untouched in pursuit of what Atatürk and the new Turkish state called *laiklik* ('secularism').

In 1924, in a move that prompted global Muslim outrage, Atatürk abolished the caliphate. In the same year he ended the authority of sharia courts. In 1926 he introduced a secular legal code on the model of Switzerland, saying:

> We must liberate our concepts of justice, our laws, and our legal institutions from the bonds, which, even though they are incompatible with the needs of our century, still hold a tight grip on us.

In these heady years of reform, the education system was purged of religion and reorganized along secular lines. Atatürk brought in the American humanist John Dewey to advise on a national educational system and founded a national Ministry of Education to safeguard a school curriculum that would train young people to be republican citizens first and foremost, with an emphasis on technical subjects. *Laiklik* from the beginning was an active project of modernization along Western lines—not just an attempt to separate religion from the state. In 1925, going beyond the secularization merely of public bodies, Atatürk closed down Sufi religious orders and Dervish lodges, religious bodies that he saw as standing in the way of this cultural project.

Laiklik was introduced by Westernized bureaucrats and military officers, not as a result of widespread social pressure, and in etymology and content it obviously borrowed from French *laïcité*. But it was also distinctive. *Laiklik* was anticlerical but it was not completely anti-religious. Revolutionaries often talked of purifying and elevating religion rather than replacing or destroying it as early French revolutionaries had. They were assisted in this by the fact that organized Islam does not require clerics, enabling them to claim that the power religious hierarchs had acquired was un-Islamic and a purer religion would result from its elimination. Additionally, in line with the controlling tendency of Turkish political history, *laiklik*, although it reduced religious control of the state, did not reduce state control of religion. On the contrary, the republic was repressive and moved to strengthen not its separation from the mosque but its control of it. Like Napoleon, Atatürk established a state department to administer religious organizations. It took over ownership of mosques and the training of imams.

Atatürk succeeded in de-Islamicizing the state but he did not succeed in doing the same to the people. Clerics who opposed secular civil law, the closure of religious orders, the ban on polygamy, and the new obligatory civil marriage staged Islamist revival attempts in the early years of the republic. They were quashed, but in the 1940s the activist secularism of the state under the continuing government of the Republican People's Party was reined in. Secularism had provoked a reaction among a newly enfranchised rural peasantry—poor, uneducated, and still attached to their folk religion—which could not be ignored. A new political movement, the Democratic Party, harnessed this sentiment, as well as popular opposition to a corrupt elite, and came to power in the first free election in the republic in 1950.

In government, the Democratic Party moved to relax secularism. All children of Muslim parents now received Islamic instruction in public schools unless opted out. Training of imams was more generously funded by the state and allowed to be conservative. Government funds were used to build thousands of new mosques. Religious NGOs began to be established and religious festivals like Ramadan were publicly celebrated again. Arabic, which had been banned in favour of Turkish, was reintroduced in religious services. All the while, in a tactic that would become typical of those seeking to weaken secularism, the government still paid extravagant lip service to Atatürk and his philosophy, even as they undermined it.

A military coup in 1960 was followed by an attempt to restore secularism in a new constitution, which also introduced a more democratic system with proportional representation, increased legal protection for human rights, and a new security council dominated by secularists from the military. Still, the great mass of the electorate remained committed in sentiment to Islam and the mismatch between the secular framework of the state and the role of Islam in national ethnic identity was a continuing tension. Elected politicians, up to and including the president, made frequent use of exclusive religious rhetoric in the course of public life. In 1980, in response to political instability and an Islamist rally calling for sharia law, the military again seized power in a coup.

While still declaring itself committed to Atatürk's philosophy, this time the military were content to see a dilution of secularism in the interests of political stability. The constitution they imposed still contained a declaration of separation of religion and state in the words of the 1961 constitution, but Islamic instruction was made compulsory in primary and secondary state schools and the identification of Turkish with Muslim was introduced into the school curriculum. Under Turgut Özal as prime minister (1983–9), then president (1989–93), government funding of Islam was massively increased, including for the printing of millions of Qurans, funding for pilgrims to Mecca, and lavish increases in mosque budgets.

The present constitution declares the Turkish republic to be *laik* in Article 2. Article 10 says 'individuals are equal without any discrimination before the law, irrespective of … philosophical belief, religion and sect, or any such considerations'. Article 24 is dedicated to 'freedom of religion and conscience' and declares 'everyone has the right to freedom of conscience, religious belief and conviction', as well as explicitly forbidding coercion into any religious practice. The same Article strives to keep religion separate from the state by declaring that no one may use religion 'in any manner whatsoever, for the purpose of personal or political influence, or for even partially basing the fundamental, social, economic, political, and legal order of the state on religious tenets'.

Constitutionally, therefore, the Turkish state has officially adopted every aspect of secularism. In spite of this, freedom and equality on grounds of religion or belief are not a feature of the republic in practice. Freedom of certain types of religion is restricted in many ways. Sufi and Alevi Muslims are not allowed to build mosques or practise their religion publicly. Although perhaps avoiding structural domination of the state by religion, through its active control of the majority religion of its people, Turkish secularism maintains not a separation of religion and state but a strong state domination over religious institutions. There is still a government ministry to control religion with the general legal purpose to carry out duties 'concerning the beliefs, worship, and ethics of Islam, enlighten the public about their religion, and administer places of worship'. It has a budget larger than that of government departments like Health or Foreign Affairs and over 100,000 employees. It trains, employs, and regulates all imams, writes their sermons, specifies the content of religious services, and micromanages the affairs of the mainstream Hanafi branch of Sunni Islam to which most Turks affiliate.

The law still allows courts to ban religious political parties but, in other ways, over sixty years of democracy in Turkey have operated substantially to reduce the secularism of the early republic. *Laiklik* had little support from the start outside the urban class and it had little intellectual foundation in Turkish culture, certainly when compared with the American and French cultures that paved the way for secularism in those countries. It was the ethnic nationalism of Atatürk's original vision rather than his secularism that bound citizens to the new Turkish state and has done ever since. By the end of the 20th century, popular and political pressure had substantially weakened secularism and, as we shall see in Chapter 7, pp. 118–21, the beneficiaries of this shift are new religious political movements, which have degraded it still further.

A completely contrasting political order, also calling itself secularism, is offered by another 20th-century republic in Asia—that of India.

India and the secularism of diversity

Indian society from ancient times has been characterized by spiritual diversity, and this has shaped how successive states across the land treated religion. During the second and first millennium BCE, spiritual life for many coalesced around a collection of scriptures called the *Vedas*, leading to the emergence of classical Hinduism. The key concept in philosophy and religion was *dharma*, which has no single-word English translation and has multiple meanings in relation to spiritual life, describing many different ways of being and living. Different individuals' and communities' interpretations of *dharma* led naturally to confessional diversity and varied schools of thought.

In the 6th century BCE, the movement that came to be called Buddhism originated in India and began its spread across Asia. Occurring at the same time as urbanization, the more worldly approach of the Buddha to questions of justice and equality included a belief that government should distance itself from or even oppose those aspects of traditional religion that were hierarchical and socially divisive. Buddhism went on to inform the laws of the Emperor Ashoka, who united India under himself in the 3rd century BCE. His laws commanded that, in matters of religion, 'One should listen to and respect the doctrines professed by others' and official policy was one of tolerance: 'All religions should reside everywhere.' Subsequent empires and kingdoms ebbed and flowed across the subcontinent for centuries, with different religion–state relationships but none so intimately or exclusively connected as in Christian Europe. Even in those parts of Indian religion that had a priestly class (*Brahmin*) there was separation between the spiritual authorities on the one hand and the political power of princes on the other. At a social level, there was most often peaceful coexistence between different Hindus, Buddhists, and Jains.

This general tradition of religious tolerance and of some practical distance between religion and state was challenged by the invasion and conquest of parts of India by Muslims. From the 13th to 19th centuries Hindu and Muslim empires and kingdoms were the dominant political orders. Some Muslim rulers were religiously oppressive, seeking to spread and enforce Islam and its rules for living. For them, there was no separation possible between authority on earth and the ultimate authority of the one God. Others were more sympathetic to the native pluralism of India. Some found resources within Islam to rule in a way that, while not impartial, was not religiously totalitarian. A tradition of Islam known as Sufism, which became strong in India, actively taught a social morality of toleration. In the 16th century one Muslim ruler named Akbar went so far as to celebrate Hindu festivals and allow Christian missionaries.

In these later centuries of religious development, further diversity was added to Indian society. A movement known as *bhakti* emerged amongst Hindus which held private religion much more important than public devotions and became popular between the 13th and 17th centuries. A whole new religion emerged in the 15th century: Sikhism, which came to reject the idea that any one religion could claim the sole truth. In the Punjab, a Sikh state under Maharaja Ranjit Singh (1780–1839), though it could not be described as secular, was highly inclusive, counting Muslims, Hindus, Sikhs, and others among its civil servants.

By the 19th century, Indian society sustained a diverse range of religions, and its history had witnessed a range of configurations of religion and the state. This long heritage of the active management of diversity provided the background conditions for secularism when it came. Further impetus to official secularism was provided by the colonial period in the continent and the fact that independence (and its associated nation building) happened to coincide with the 20th-century heyday of secularism.

The colonial power in India was Britain. As a result of a series of trade deals, political negotiations, and military incursions in the 18th and early 19th centuries, it secured control over the whole of India by 1858. At home, the British state supported an established church but, faced away from its shores with deep-rooted religious diversity, it adopted a different policy. The priorities in India were commerce and trade, and the colonial state did not seek to convert people to or from any religion (although, at the insistence of the British Parliament, it did allow Christian missionaries). Instead, a new equality before the law for Indians regardless of religion was introduced and a number of officially recognized parallel family and personal laws for each different religious community. This regime held throughout the 19th and early 20th centuries.

Growing anti-colonialism led eventually to a negotiated withdrawal of Britain from the subcontinent and its partition in 1947 into two new states: Pakistan and India. India was a secular state with no official religion. Two prominent independence campaigners in particular made this so: Jawaharlal Nehru (1889–1964) and Mohandas Gandhi (1869–1948). From the 1920s to the 1940s they were leaders in the Indian National Congress, the main movement for independence (see Figure 3).

3. Nehru and Gandhi—two faces of Indian secularism—together at a 1946 meeting where the secularism of India was discussed.

Gandhi was committed to religious tolerance and pluralism. He himself was inspired by Western philosophy as well as diverse Indian thought and had worked during the struggle for independence to bring together Hindus, Muslims, Christians, the non-religious, and others in opposing the British. Writing in 1927 of the future he sought, he said:

> I do not expect India of my dream to develop one religion...to be wholly Hindu, or wholly Christian, or wholly Muslim, but I want it to be wholly tolerant, with its religious working side by side with one another.

This concern for pluralism led him to favour secularism. The journal *Harijan* reported him in 1947 as saying that:

> In the India for whose fashioning he had worked all his life every man enjoyed equality of status, whatever his religion was. The state was bound to be wholly secular. He went so far as to say that no denominational institution in it should enjoy state patronage. All subjects would thus be equal in the eye of the law.

A Hindu nationalist assassinated Gandhi before he could see the new India properly established but Nehru did survive to see it and was prime minster of the new nation from its foundation until his death in 1964. Unlike Gandhi, he was not religious. He was strongly influenced by the thought of Enlightenment Europe, especially of Britain and France, saying that organized religion 'filled [him] with horror'. He saw state secularism as the only pathway to modernity for a new nation.

In 1949 the Constituent Assembly charged with creating the Indian constitution adopted a text that included a declaration of what the state wished to secure for its people. Among the aims were 'LIBERTY of thought, expression, belief, faith and worship, EQUALITY of status and of opportunity'. It wasn't until 1976 that the 42nd Amendment to the Constitution added secularism to the list, but the original contained all the aspects of secularism and was referred to as secular from its adoption onwards.

Article 25 stated that, 'subject to public order, morality and health...all persons are equally entitled to freedom of conscience and the right freely to profess, practise and propagate religion'. Notwithstanding this freedom, the state was given power to make laws to regulate secular activities associated with religions and 'for social welfare and reform or the throwing open of Hindu religious institutions of a public character to all classes and sections'. This was targeted at improving the conditions of those deemed untouchable in India's caste system and established from the beginning that Indian secularism did not rule out potential intervention by the state in the religious practices of the majority religion in the interests of social equality. This characteristic of Indian secularism has been retained.

Article 26 gave any religion and denomination freedom to organize and 'to manage its own affairs in matters of religion', and Article 27 provided that no person could be 'compelled to pay any taxes...for the promotion or maintenance of any particular religion or religious denomination'.

In general, the principles of the constitution creating secularism have operated well to protect freedom and equality but the failure of one of them in particular has called Indian secularism into question. In place of the community-specific laws put in place by the British, Article 44 of the constitution declared: 'The State shall endeavour to secure for the citizens a uniform civil code throughout the territory of India.' In 1954, civil marriage and divorce became available to all Indians, and this provided for the first time an opportunity for the matter of marriage and associated questions like inheritance to be dealt with by the secular law rather than under a community-specific code. Although Nehru was personally committed to the fuller introduction of a uniform civil code, however, there were no successes beyond this reform.

In the decades following independence, the settled situation became one in which Muslims were subject to one personal law and other Indians were subject to a secularized Hindu personal law. In 1985, the Supreme Court called for a uniform civil code when it found in favour of a Muslim woman, Shah Bano, in her claim for maintenance from an ex-husband who had divorced her unilaterally (as permitted by the Muslim personal law). But the Indian Parliament, instead of pursuing such a course, actually changed the law to ensure that Muslim personal law would still be respected and women not given any benefits that it did not allow them. In the controversy that followed, many Indians supported reform that would introduce one law for all on grounds of sex equality and secularism. On the other hand, many Muslims protested that a uniform code would be anti-secular, as it would impose Hindu values on Muslims under the guise of civil law, replacing the traditional practices of polygamy and unilateral divorce that a tolerant and pluralist state should protect. This claim, and the support for it offered by Parliament in practice, prompted criticism that a secularism that would preserve pluralism at such a cost was 'pseudo-secularism'. This controversy continues and illustrates the unique social tensions that Indian secularism must mediate.

As in Turkey, specific laws seek to protect Indian secularism from the political use of religion. Under section 123 of the Representation of the People Act, courts can disqualify candidates for election who are 'promoting or attempting to promote feelings of enmity or hatred between different classes of the citizens of India on grounds of religion'. Still, non-political religious tension has been responsible for much inter-communal violence in India. Sectarian rioters killed 3,000 Sikhs in 1984 but only a handful of them were arrested and tried. Muslims have faced mob violence, most shockingly in 2002, when 10,000 rioters destroyed hundreds of mosques, destroyed 20,000 homes, and killed 1000 in Gujarat. No one was arrested. Hindus aggrieved by the perception that the secular state is biased against them have proved to be a frequent source of disorder, and the avowed secular state has often failed to bring them to justice.

Indian secularism rejects not just theocracy but any formal links between state and religious structures and is similar to this extent to secularism in the US or in France. But if American secularism arose to protect religion from the state and French secularism to protect the individual from religion, Indian secularism has different aims. It seeks to protect people with different beliefs from each other. The policies and practices in pursuit of this aim in some states even extend to positive discrimination in favour of some religious minorities in the state education system. This secularism is non-sectarian but positively values religious pluralism at the same time as affirming a national unity. Although it has experienced tensions and violence, India has held together a nation of 1.25 billion diverse believers in democracy and relative peace. Secularism has greatly assisted that unlikely success.

International secularism

In 1948 a *Universal Declaration of Human Rights* was proclaimed by the United Nations, having been drafted by a commission chaired by the American Eleanor Roosevelt and including members from all over the world, including Russia, Europe, Chile, China, and Lebanon. Although eight nations abstained, none voted against it. In 1976, having been ratified by a sufficient number of states, it became international law. Article 18 contains a strong assertion of freedom of religion or belief:

> Everyone has the right to freedom of thought, conscience and religion; this right includes freedom to change his religion or belief, and freedom, either alone or in community with others and in public or private, to manifest his religion or belief in teaching, practice, worship and observance.

The Declaration's preamble eschewed unshared theological claims, rooting itself entirely in pragmatic ground, claiming that 'recognition of the inherent dignity and of the equal and inalienable rights of all members of the human family is the foundation of freedom, justice and peace in the world'. It is a peak of secularist achievement. It asserts the principle of freedom of religion or belief; those of many religions and non-religious world views had a hand in its production; its principles of pluralism are the antithesis of theocracy. It earned the corresponding ire of many anti-secularists the world over—and still does.

In the second half of the 20th century, the international political pressure on states to respect the rule of law and the international system was significant. The superpowers of the US and the Soviet Union were both *seen* as secular states in one way or another, as were other states with global significance like France. States seen as success stories of modernization like India or Turkey had adopted secularism. All this added up to a certain pressure on states, if they wished to join the new community of nations, to pay at least lip service to freedom of religion or belief. In 1966, the *International Covenant on Civil and Political Rights* established a form of words they could use in their own laws, and many did. Secularism came to be seen by many as an essential part of unstoppable progressive political change, as inevitable and desirable as welfare economies and liberal democracy.

The biggest shock to this assumption was the Islamist revolution in Iran in 1979, which overturned what had been seen as an emerging regional exemplar of secularism. Optimistic secularists could see even this in the last decades of the 20th century as no more than a blip, but the strain that the secularism of states in Asia like Bangladesh have come under more recently offers a mounting challenge to the idea that it can provide a successful political order everywhere. As the 21st century gets under way, the picture seems suddenly more complex. Secularism is contested from all quarters and its opponents are voicing criticisms some of its supporters find difficult to counter. At the same time, secularism is winning new adherents in many parts of the world as populations subject to strong religious sanctions see it still as one of the essential aspects of modernity, to be embraced as an instrument of both personal liberation and social peace. To understand the advocates and opponents of secularism, let's turn now to the arguments they make.

Chapter 4
The case for secularism

All the states that have adopted a secular system have done it in their own way, as we have witnessed in our survey of just a few examples. Since this book is only a very short introduction, we haven't looked in detail at most of the states in the world and not at all at Africa. Nonetheless, we've seen quite different arrangements all under the name of secularism. The secular systems of different states have varied according to the nature of their own particular society and their religious, cultural, and political history. Even so, the same types of arguments have been used each time to advance secularism as the best religion–state arrangement to provide freedom, equality, peace, and democracy in a modern society.

Individual freedom

The argument for secularism based on individual freedom is rooted in a particular understanding of human dignity. It starts from the assumption that, as far as is possible, we want to be free to make up our own minds about important questions. This includes questions of religion or belief, and imposing opinions on individuals by state sanction is a violation of this freedom.

This view of the human being and what are the best conditions for human flourishing is strongly associated with the liberal humanist tradition of philosophy. In 1859 the British writer and statesman John Stuart Mill (1806–73) published *On Liberty*, which went on to become a liberal classic. In Chapter One he articulated what became known as the *harm principle*: 'The only purpose for which power can be rightfully exercised over any member of a civilized community, against his will, is to prevent harm to others.' This political principle is defensible on many grounds but one of Mill's own justifications was a certain view of human nature. In his essay he says he is addressing 'the wellbeing of mankind'. His view is that, 'Among the works of man, which human life is rightly employed in perfecting and beautifying, the first in importance surely is man himself.'

Mill encouraged his readers to value not just experience, but also the discussion and examination of experience, so we can make our choices reflectively, developing 'the human faculties of perception, judgment, discriminative feeling, mental activity, and ... moral preference'. He encouraged readers to ask 'what would allow the best and highest in me to have fair play, and enable it to grow and thrive?' so we can become 'more valuable' to ourselves and 'therefore capable of being more valuable to others'. He believed that 'human nature is not a machine ... but a tree, which requires to grow and develop itself on all sides'.

All this is only possible with freedom of conscience, thought, and religion, and these freedoms have a correspondingly high value in the social and political thought of any liberal. This value has very strongly informed the argument from freedom that is advanced for secularism.

It is not only on liberal humanist grounds that the argument for individual freedom can be made. An argument for human dignity based on freedom to choose can also be made on religious grounds. We saw in the history of religion and politics in Europe that Baptists developed a belief that the only valid faith is one acquired in the context of freedom. In 1612 the Baptist Helwys published *A Short Declaration on the Mystery of Iniquity* which affirmed that the king, as a mere man, had no right to make laws on matters reserved to God and that as long as men and women obeyed all 'humane laws' made by the king, then:

> our Lord the King can require no more: for men's religion to God is between God and themselves. The King shall not answer for it. Neither may the King be judge between God and man.

In our own time, referencing multiple verses from the Christian Bible in support of it, Article XVII in the 2000 edition of *The Baptist Faith and Message* has restated this belief:

> God alone is Lord of the conscience, and He has left it free from the doctrines and commandments of men which are contrary to His Word or not contained in it. Church and state should be separate. The state owes to every church protection and full freedom in the pursuit of its spiritual ends. In providing for such freedom no ecclesiastical group or denomination should be favoured by the state more than others...The gospel of Christ contemplates spiritual means alone for the pursuit of its ends. The state has no right to impose penalties for religious opinions of any kind. The state has no right to impose taxes for the support of any form of religion. A free church in a free state is the Christian ideal, and this implies the right of free and unhindered access to God on the part of all men, and the right to form and propagate opinions in the sphere of religion without interference by the civil power.

There may be no other religious denomination quite so firm in its conviction that God himself is a secularist, but there are resources in almost every religious tradition to support the 'freedom' argument for secularism. Muslims who want to support it point to the first sentence of 2:256 of the Quran that 'There is no compulsion in religion.' Most religious interpreters of this phrase throughout history have read it as meaning simply that Islam is so obvious that you should not even need to explain it to people. But taken together with other parts of the Quran in which God says that he could have made everyone a Muslim if he had wanted to, but didn't do so, others have used this verse to make the same argument as the Baptists. It was interpreted by some Muslim rulers in India and by some Ottoman sultans as supporting a plural approach to the government of their territories and is used by secularist Muslims today to support the freedom argument. Drawing on a Hindu perspective of religion as an individual matter, Gandhi said:

> I swear by my religion. I will die for it. But it is my personal affair...The state would look after your secular welfare, health, communications, foreign relations, currency and so on, but not your or my religion. That is everybody's personal concern.

In the language of universal human rights, in principle accessible to all people, we have already seen how it is this argument that frames the secularist insistence in the *Universal Declaration of Human Rights* that everyone should have 'freedom, either alone or in community with others and in public or private, to manifest his religion or belief in teaching, practice, worship and observance'.

Fairness

Many arguments for secularism are characterized by the claim that it is *fairer* than the alternatives. This argument starts with the idea that every individual in a society should be treated equally, regardless of their religious or philosophical convictions and not be disadvantaged or privileged because of them. If I am a Muslim in a state that restricts university education to Buddhists, or a humanist in a state that restricts employment rights to Muslims, or a Christian in a state that restricts political office to atheists, I am being treated unfairly. Again, this is an argument strongly associated with the liberal tradition of political thought and relies on an idea in political philosophy known as the 'social contract'.

At the time of the Enlightenment we saw thinkers applying themselves to the question of how government could be justified. 'Social contract' thinking emerged as one such justification. In order to avoid disruptive and dangerous anarchy, the argument went, we make an agreement with each other and with government that we will accept our own liberty being curbed to the extent that it is necessary to guarantee the liberty of others. We all benefit from this because it provides a better situation than the unstable alternative. The most famous exposition of this is Rousseau's *Of the Social Contract*, which had such great influence on the French revolutionaries.

Whether in the work of Rousseau or elsewhere, the 'social contract' is, of course, not a real contract—none of us is ever asked to sign it or have a personal say in its content. How then, can we be sure that what we are tacitly promising to abide by is fair?

In his 1971 book *A Theory of Justice*, the political philosopher John Rawls (1921–2002) came up with a vivid way to test the fairness of the social contract. He suggested a metaphor of a 'veil of ignorance'. When we decide what a fair society will look like, we have to imagine we are behind this veil of ignorance as to what our own position will be in that society. Behind the veil, as Rawls said:

> no one knows his place in society, his class position or social status, nor does anyone know his fortune in the distribution of natural assets and abilities, his intelligence, strength, and the like. I shall even assume that the parties do not know their conceptions of the good or their special psychological propensities.

Starting from this position of ignorance, Rawls says, we will naturally choose principles for organizing our society that do not unduly favour any one group on grounds like wealth or talents. The thought experiment gives us a way of deciding what is fair on a social level, grounded in empathy and concern for others as well as for ourselves.

It's obvious how this argument can be used to support secularism. Behind the veil of ignorance we do not know whether we will be religious or not, and if we will, whether we will be Muslims, Hindus, Buddhists, Christians, Jews, Zoroastrians, or whatever. In this situation, the state configuration we would naturally prefer is a secular one. That is the only way we know we will not be persecuted and will have the freedom to make our own choices. If we privilege one religious identity or one set of religious beliefs for public funding or preferment, we would run the risk of disadvantaging ourselves if we turn out not to have that identity or those beliefs. If we allow one religion to dictate the common laws of a shared society on abortion or other life issues, we would risk having our own choices denied. If we allow the state to provide religious instruction in its schools of only one type, our children may be indoctrinated against our will.

Added force is given to social contract thinking about secularism by the fact that our religion or world view—unlike some of our other characteristics—may well change over the course of our lives so that we really cannot be sure from one year to the next what our beliefs will be. A young person with devout Salafi Muslim beliefs may be perfectly content in totalitarian Saudi Arabia, but if she finds herself questioning her youthful beliefs in middle age, rejecting them, and becoming non-religious, her society will suddenly become a lot less comfortable.

The idea of a 'social contract' is most fully expressed in the Enlightenment tradition of thought (Rawls himself was a liberal and a humanist) and began as a rejection of the static, divinely ordained models of the state promoted by Christianity. But versions of it can be found in other cultures and traditions. In the *Suttapitaka*, an ancient Buddhist text, the story is told of how government by a king originated because human beings needed a way to guarantee the rules that they had developed to live with each other. This view of the social order as determined by people rather than being divinely mandated was an alternative to the hierarchical view of Hindu Brahmins just as the social contract view was an alternative to that of Christian Europe.

Some Christians also find resources in their sacred texts to support the idea that the business of political life in this world is subject to a different set of obligations from that which relates to God and religion. Two stories in particular are used. In the first, some men try to trick Jesus into sedition against the authority of the Roman emperor by asking him whether Jews like them should pay a poll tax levied by the authorities. They hope he will say no and compromise himself. But Jesus tells them to show him a coin and asks them whose head and name are on it. When the men reply that the head and name are those of the emperor, Jesus replies, 'Give the emperor what is the emperor's and God what is God's.' In the second story, Jesus is captured by Jewish religious officials and brought before Pilate, the Roman magistrate. The Jewish officials want him charged for illegally claiming to be king. When Pilate tries to determine whether Jesus really has claimed this, Jesus replies, 'My kingdom is not of this world. If it were, my servants would have been fighting to prevent me being delivered to the Jews.'

The obvious interpretations of the two stories are that in the first, Jesus avoided entrapment with a clever answer, which at the same time exposed his accusers' own complicity with the Roman state, whose coins they carried. In the second, Jesus is saying that he is plainly not a king, or he would not be in front of a magistrate. However, Christians who wish to do so can interpret them both as implying delineation between the domain of Jesus and Christianity, on the one hand, and the mundane sphere of the state and the magistrate, on the other.

It is not just Buddhists and Christians who have theological resources to support the idea of fairness but other religions too, especially where their ethics are based on compassion and empathy.

Peace

Arguments to do with fairness and freedom are not entirely
distinctive of any one religious or non-religious tradition and are
in principle accessible and persuasive to those of any tradition.
Even so, they will not convince everyone. 'Why should I promote
the freedom of the heretic?' a believer may ask. 'Her views are a
blasphemy and my unshakeable faith tells me I am correct.' 'Why
should I allow a Muslim to worship freely?' the atheist communist
may ask. 'Her views are based on fairy tales, empirically falsifiable,
and should be eliminated, not sponsored.' Such questions will
always come from those who believe that their own ideals should
be the ones that rule society, even to the extent of becoming the
state's own aims and ends.

In response to such critics, the case for secularism shifts onto more
pragmatic ground. It is the best way to organize a society made up
of potentially conflicting groups defined by religion or belief.
History tells us how the attempts by various states to prescribe and
proscribe religions in Europe led to conflict, war, and gross
inhumanity. It tells us how Muslims and Hindus in India were at
odds for centuries and the ways in which persecution and
oppression fuelled destabilizing enmity and hatred. We can all see
today that differences of identity and conviction spill over easily
into conflict. A political order where coercive and intolerant
religion is in authority exacerbates and amplifies that conflict.

Conflict may not mean outright violence. Peace is not just
the absence of war, and other conflicts should count in our
calculations. The resentment that is fomented when some are
treated less favourably than others, discriminated against or
privileged in their access to public services, or preferred for state
responsibilities should all count. The prejudice and hostility
generated by these circumstances may or may not lead to violence
and physical harm, but it certainly leads to a society not at peace

and ease with itself. In contrast, a secular state can take the sting out of many potential areas of conflict. As Gandhi said:

> What conflict of interest can there be between Hindus and Muslims in the matter of revenue, sanitation, police, justice, or the use of public conveniences? The difference can only be in religious usage and observance with which a secular state has no concern.

This pragmatic argument for secularism is not immune to objection. Some religious believers will never put up with others, and waves of violent religious revival will disturb even the fairest of political settlements. Secularism itself will generate resentment and violence from those who want their own religion to dominate. But in the final analysis, secularists making this argument claim that this is more containable than a war of everyone against everyone else. In general, all parties benefit. To make a war of all against all less likely, we must have a neutral state as the only way to deal with inevitable social diversity.

Modernity and democracy

The word 'modernity' is used to describe the evolving social condition of the West, and later the whole world, in the centuries following the end of Christendom in Europe. The rejection of tradition and the pursuit of individual freedom and happiness and human progress, especially through science as a method with technology as its fruits: all these are aspects of what sociologists call modernity. For the advocates of secularism, there is a long tradition of arguing that it is the only modern way to run a state—the only political system compatible with modernity, which will allow a society to benefit from modernity's advantages.

In the case of revolutionary France and Atatürk's infant republic we saw that arguments quite different from those of fairness and freedom were advanced for secularism. Arguments in these situations were arguments for modernization—for the clearing away of the ancient rubble of religious institutions, and religion itself, so that society might make progress. This argument is one of liberation. It rests on the idea that, in order for societies to become modern, they need to escape from ancient restrictive codes of ethics and theocracy. And it is not just an argument about societies—it also claims that personal flourishing of individuals depends on the same process of liberation. In this sense it overlaps with the argument for individual freedom.

In India, Nehru called secularism one of the 'pillars of modernity'. He believed a democratic republic could only be secular, and in many places the argument for modernity has been wound up in this additional argument about democracy. Only if there is an open and universally accessible public realm in which people of all different religions can feel welcome can we all discuss our social views together in shared and equal citizenship. Religious beliefs expressed in public debates are not in principle open to all; they cannot hope to be the basis of a shared understanding between citizens. And if we don't have that shared understanding, we can't have democracy. Where the state has a religious character, unshared by many citizens, this will lead to their feeling excluded from the body politic. Even if it is only a nominal religious character, it will at the very best still engender a hypocrisy and doublethink that is at odds with the openness required by democracy. In Norway, the established nature of the church entailed a requirement that a certain number of Cabinet members must be Lutherans, and in the Republic of Ireland the constitution requires that the president must make an oath to God. In both countries, people have performed these roles and conformed when it has been known that they were not in fact believers.

This argument about democracy is in a sense a version of the pragmatic argument. Conflict sparked by irreconcilable differences is replaced by a fair and equal democratic participation that can replace violence with debate. At the foundation of this argument is an acknowledgement of the inevitable diversity of beliefs that are found in any society. In theory, it might be fair and peaceful and democratic to have a non-secular state if every member of society had the same beliefs. Such societies may have existed in the past—religiously homogeneous colonies in what became British North America, for example. Today, however, no society is homogeneous in that way.

A cumulative case

The arguments made for secularism appeal to very different audiences. Devout religious believers are unlikely to respond to the liberation argument, but they may see the appeal of the argument for personal autonomy. An anti-religious bigot may be repelled by the argument for fairness but accept the pragmatic argument. Like all responses to political questions of complexity, the case for secularism is cumulative and not a single knockdown proposition. Of necessity, it is also a case that deals with what is the best possible outcome, not the perfect outcome. Living in society always involves compromise and mutual accommodation, and a perfect outcome for all in a complicated and diverse society does not exist. Nonetheless, one thing all these arguments do is to assert the value of an impartial state that mediates the differences of its citizens. This, of course, is not the only possible view of the role of the state, and anti-secularists, when they come to make their arguments against secularism, often start with a very different view. It is to their arguments that we now turn.

Chapter 5
The case against secularism

The case for secularism is relatively simple and, though secularists may differ in the emphasis they give to different arguments, by and large they agree on the core of it. Opposition to secularism is more diverse. For a start, arguments against secularism come from both defensive and offensive positions and vary accordingly. Opponents of secularism in the age when it was hypothetical made arguments to defend the religious status quo. Many of these are still used today. Since the institution of secularism as a state system, new arguments have come from secularism's critics, and these have a different character, targeted as they are at an ideology in power. It adds further complexity that many critics of secularism seek to modify its content and change its definition rather than to oppose it completely.

Nations under god

Governments may align themselves with a religious establishment and deny freedom and equality to adherents of other religions for many reasons, but the oldest and most obvious reason to do so is that those in power believe that their religion is true. If you believe this *and* your religion is one of the monotheistic ones that make exclusive truth claims, you can easily think that your state should be entirely based on your religion alone. Such 'nations under God' are at odds with all three aspects of secularism. There is no question of the separation of religious institutions from state institutions: they are one and the same. Freedom of conscience for non-adherents of the state's religion, if it is provided at all, is provided only insofar as the religion of the state concedes it. In place of equal treatment, the state favours its own religion in its dealings with society.

Strictly speaking, the word 'theocracy' describes only states that claim to be governed *directly* by the divine as expressed either through an individual or through sacred texts. It was used in the ancient world to describe the way Jews saw God's words as laws and ancient Jews are one of the few examples of a genuine theocracy. Like theocracies are states where the political order is seen as being under God and mandated by God but delegated to earthly bodies. The England of Henry VIII or the empire of the Ottoman sultan and caliph are two examples we have encountered. Somewhat different in character are states where one religion is officially preferred and privileged as the state's official religion, though no longer seen as divinely mandated.

There are few pure theocracies in today's world and have never been many. There are equally few delegated theocracies, though there have been many more in the past. There are many states with an official religion, almost all Christian or Muslim, but these vary enormously in what official recognition of a religion means in practice.

Islamic states

The religion of Islam originated in modern day Saudi Arabia in the 7th century CE. Muslims believe a man named Mohammed received revelations from the God of the Jews and Christians as God's last prophet and that these revelations explained to humanity the way to live for all time. Mohammed was a political leader as well as a religious one, and Muslims believe that, in his lifetime, he presided over a genuine theocracy.

They believe the words of God to Mohammed transmitted over two decades are recorded in a text known as the *Quran*. Secondary sources of Islam are the *hadith*, sayings attributed to Mohammed and reports of his acts. Taken together, some Muslims believe these texts provide not just religious instruction but a manual for government.

Ayatollah Khomeini, the anti-secularist revolutionary who became Supreme Leader under Iran's Islamic constitution of 1979, wrote *Islamic Government* in 1970. Part conspiracy theory (it claims the Jews and British have a secret plan to undermine the Muslim world) and part revolutionary manifesto, it is a modern restatement of the theocratic case. Dismissing the idea that Islam is, 'like Christianity', merely 'a collection of injunctions pertaining to man's relation to God', Khomeini asserted that, through Mohammed, God:

> instituted laws and practices for all human affairs... In just the same way that there are laws setting forth the duties of worship for man, so too there are laws, practices, and norms for the affairs of society and government. Islamic law is a progressive, evolving, and comprehensive system... There is not a single topic in human life for which Islam has not provided instructions and established a norm.

Khomeini went on to specify in broad terms the nature of true Islamic political order—rule according to the sharia by a government kept in check by a senior Islamic scholar—and exhorted Muslims to take up the challenge of establishing it:

> The entire system of government and administration, together with necessary laws, lies ready for you. If the administration of the country calls for taxes, Islam has made the necessary provision; and if laws are needed, Islam has established them all... Everything is ready and waiting.

In fact, today's self-described Islamic states offer a range of very different constitutional arrangements, not just one system. In two of them—Saudi Arabia and the Maldives—state and religion are utterly indistinguishable. Every citizen must be a Muslim. The sharia is either enforced directly or is the basis of additional civil and criminal laws. Public practice of religions other than the state's Islam is forbidden. Criticism of the religion is forbidden, as is leaving it. These crimes carry penalties of imprisonment, torture, and death. Mosques and imams are controlled by the state, and the police enforce religious practices such as fasting and religious dress.

In other Islamic states, like Iran, Pakistan, or Malaysia, the state does not require every citizen to be a Muslim but does regulate and police the religious life of its citizens who *are* Muslims. They severely limit the civic participation of non-Muslims, sometimes banning them from public office or military service, and restrict the practice of religions other than Islam. They either enforce sharia directly as law or give it a place in the legal system and often control religious institutions, licensing imams or mosques.

In other Islamic states, political authorities control and sponsor Islamic institutions but do not get involved in *enforcing* religion to the same extent. Governments like those of Bahrain or Jordan are more separate from religious authority and religious institutions than the government of Iran. In such countries, religious institutions also have greater independence from the state than the mosques of Saudi Arabia. Their laws do not include sharia to as great an extent and include secular aspects that others would think incompatible with sharia, especially in relation to sex equality. Still, Islam is seen as the foundation of the political order.

Islamic states may be republics, monarchies, or oligarchies; they may have democratic elements to their constitutions or be virtual dictatorships. Ayatollah Khomeini claimed that Islam offered a complete system of government, but this diversity reveals that claim as mere rhetoric. Even in Iran there are non-Islamic influences in the constitution and in the practice of government.

Once in power, Khomeini himself was flexible in his principles, even claiming that sharia could be overruled in certain circumstances. Islam is not such a pure alternative to secularism as it is vaunted to be. Added to this, there is often a strong whiff of realpolitik around the declaration of a state as Islamic. Islamic identity gives legitimacy to regimes in societies where religious affiliation is strong: it wins the loyalty of the people and galvanizes the material and intellectual support of religious institutions for the regime. Cynicism as much as piety may explain this alternative to secularism.

Established churches

A Christian case for a sort of theocracy was advanced against the secularism of John Locke by Jonas Proast (c.1640–1710). Proast was a Church of England priest who published responses to Locke's works on toleration. He believed that Protestantism was the true religion mandated by God and that Roman Catholicism was a false religion. He argued that, this being so, civil authorities should be able to use force in seeking to promote the one and suppress the other for the good of citizens. He asserted that matters of religion have an impact on society in this world and so rejected the ideas that there was a clear divide between the spheres of state and church and that state power should never be directed towards religious ends. If the power of the state could assist in saving men's souls and spreading truth (and Proast said that it could, denying Locke's claim that coercion in matters of faith was never effective), then the state had a duty to use that power.

None of today's officially Christian nation states is a full theocracy, and they occupy a wide range of positions making further or closer approaches to the three aspects of secularism. In all of them, of course, state and religious institutions are linked in some way. In some, religious institutions dominate, for example, state provision of education or health. In others the state dominates the religious institutions, regulating their business. In many, the two sets of institutions are entirely autonomous, linked in name only, and have little practical influence on each other. In all such states there is some legal preference for those of a certain religion in certain aspects of life, and in some that preference can extend to many aspects of public life, but in most that preference is confined to a few public offices or state employments. In some, freedom of conscience and religion is granted to all on the same basis, with no distinction; in others, there are limitations on the freedom of conscience of those who are not of the state's religion.

The UK offers a good case study of an established church as an alternative to secularism.

We have already seen how Henry VIII made the monarch the head of the church in England. This is still the case, but it is no longer compulsory in England to be a member of the national church (in Scotland it never was). From the late 17th to late 19th centuries, first all non-Anglican Protestants, then Roman Catholics, Jews, and the non-religious acquired equality before the law with Anglicans in a gradual process of increasing 'toleration'. In Ireland and Wales, where Anglicans were a clear minority, the Church of England was 'disestablished': in Ireland in 1871 and in Wales in 1920. Secularist campaigns failed, however, to achieve disestablishment in England or official secularism in any part of the UK.

In the late 20th century, when devolved national governments were set up in Wales and Scotland, they were secular in character, but the Church of England remains the established church in England. The state formally appoints its bishops, some of whom sit in the UK Parliament and vote on legislation; the monarch is legally obliged to be a member of it; national occasions and ceremonies are presided over by its priests. It runs a quarter of state schools in England and is a fierce lobbyist in favour of religious privilege, such as laws allowing religious parents priority access to certain state-funded schools, mandating Christian worship in all state schools, and allowing religious discrimination in the provision of public services. The UN and other human rights bodies have highlighted these features of the state as incompatible with freedom of conscience and with equal treatment.

Although it is still officially a Christian state, nonetheless, there are secular elements to the state and government in England. The slow relaxation of the social, civic, and political disadvantages suffered by those not in membership of the Churches of England or Scotland was an attempt to reduce the burden of an established church without the disruptive act of disestablishment that would threaten entrenched elites. In the 21st century, less than a fifth of the UK population say they are members of the Church of England, and less than 2 per cent of the population attend its services on any given week. UK society is diverse and mostly non-religious, and government cannot in practice avoid that fact. Religious concerns do not predominate in government, which maintains a secular ethic in the vast majority of its business, the role of the church ebbs and flows with the personalities of politicians involved, and equality laws deriving from Europe have been incorporated into UK law in a way that has reduced and in some cases outlawed discrimination on grounds of religion or belief.

Eighteenth-century apologists for establishment, like ancient Romans, thought it acceptable for individuals to have their own beliefs as long as they outwardly confessed those of the state when prompted. Modern defenders of Christian establishments are not so extreme. Given the necessity to concede at least some human rights to those of different religions and beliefs, today's advocates of a religious basis to the state couch their support for church establishment in different terms. They argue that a 'hospitable'

Christianity is the best foundation for the state. In 2006 the Anglican Bishop Michael Nazir Ali said:

> British society is based on a Christian vision and Christian values...And this is the best basis to have an open and welcoming society where other people can make their contribution...If there's a clearer Christian basis to society which is acknowledged, the result will be a better basis for a more inclusive society, a better basis for welcoming people than a kind of secularist lowest common denominator.

Queen Elizabeth II went further in 2012 in a speech in Lambeth Palace, the home of the archbishop of Canterbury, when she spoke of 'the significant position of the Church of England in our nation's life':

> The concept of our established Church is occasionally misunderstood and, I believe, commonly under-appreciated. Its role is not to defend Anglicanism to the exclusion of other religions. Instead, the Church has a duty to protect the free practice of all faiths in this country...gently and assuredly, the Church of England has created an environment for other faith communities and indeed people of no faith to live freely.

This 'duty' of the Church of England is, of course, not a real legal duty, and it is not clear quite what is meant by the phrase here, but the gist of it is obvious. It is an attempt to construct what is known as a 'tolerant' or 'hospitable' establishment—to say that a liberal Christian state, rather than a secular one, is best placed to mediate the diversity of contemporary society. England is at one extreme of the spectrum of nations with established churches—it is, for example, the only one with religious representatives in its legislature. But it is far from egregious. Denmark's national church is also strongly established. It is governed by a government department that makes decisions on church building, its statutes are made by Parliament as part of public law, its forms of worship are authorized by royal decree, and its clergy are appointed by the state. The church receives public funding in grants as well as through a church tax collected from citizens by the state.

The mere existence of functioning Islamic and Christian states provides a challenge to the 'modernity and democracy' arguments for secularism. Iran has nuclear technology, Denmark has democratic political institutions, and England has a vibrant civil society. Secularism may not be the essential pillar of modernity that Nehru claimed. Going further, do freedom of religion or belief and equal treatment truly depend on the separation of church and state? The pragmatic accommodation made by many established churches to freedom of religion or belief, which has led to their supporting rights for others, may suggest not. The question is further complicated by the fact that, while they are not officially secular, many states with established churches have developed a secular political ethic in practice. The state may own an official religion but in relation to secularism's other two aspects, it may be more secular than states with no official religion.

Perhaps. But secularists will still say that as long as one religion has official status, the citizens of a state cannot be truly equal. A valued guest in a 'hospitable' establishment is nonetheless not at home. In every state with an established church there is discrimination of some sort and even where they have begun to treat religious people equally, they often continue discrimination against the non-religious. It is also true that, in those established church states that have moved furthest towards freedom and equal treatment, such as Sweden or Norway, this progress has necessitated at least an attenuation of establishment, if not complete separation. Establishment may be compatible with growing freedom and fairness in the short term, but perhaps not forever.

Nations under Marx

Theocrats want to use the state to promote and defend their religion. It wasn't until the 20th century that atheists offered examples of the flip side of the coin.

The political thinker Karl Marx (1818–83) thought religion would naturally disappear as humanity progressed towards what he called 'upper-stage Communism': a global society where everyone was equal, without distinctions of class. His ideas inspired Vladimir Lenin (1870–1924), first leader (1917–24) of the Soviet Union, set up under Marxist principles in Russia after a violent revolution. His interpretation of Marxism—Marxism-Leninism—was influential on all future Communist states. Lenin believed that the state was justified in actively removing barriers that stood in the way of humanity's destiny rather than just waiting for nature to take its course. Religions were one such barrier because they were untrue (and so made people ignorant) and anti-socialist (because they taught workers to be satisfied with their exploitation in hope of better treatment in an afterlife).

Adopting the same tactics as the French ultra-revolutionaries in the 1790s, Lenin's regime confiscated the property of the Russian Orthodox Church, which had supported the absolutist monarchy of Russia just as the Roman Catholic Church had supported that of France. Seminaries and religious institutions were closed down and clerics persecuted. An official doctrine of atheism was expounded in schools and other state social institutions. The Soviet Union lasted for over seventy years, and over the course of its history there were different schools of thought on what the policy towards religion ought to be. Some argued that religion should be left to its natural fate with no need for state persecution. Others argued it must be exterminated by force. At this extreme end of the spectrum was the Communist Party organization known as 'The League of the Militant Godless', led by Yemelyan Yaroslavsky (1878–1943), which was active from the 1920s to the 1940s in trying to persuade and coerce people away from the religions of Islam, Christianity, and Judaism. It sent state-sponsored atheist missionaries to both urban and rural workers and issued periodicals and other pamphlets satirizing and condemning both religious beliefs and religious believers. All members of the Communist Party youth wing were required to join the League and in 1930 it adopted a five-year plan to eliminate religion entirely. Generally, however, persecution of the religious came in waves in the Soviet Union, and never again grew as intense as in these early days.

Albania was the first Communist state to officially declare itself atheist rather than secular under the regime of Enver Hoxha (1908–85). In 1976 the constitution declared, 'The State recognises no religion, and supports atheist propaganda in order to implant a scientific materialistic worldview in the people.' Religion was banned, with prison sentences for those found in possession of religious writings or artefacts. In the same year Cuba also declared itself officially a materialist state, amending its constitution to say that the state 'bases its activity on, and educates the people in, the scientific materialist concept of the universe'.

These avowedly atheist states were short-lived. Both in Albania and Cuba, the collapse of the Soviet Union in 1989 precipitated constitutional changes that led to the state again being declared 'secular' rather than atheistic.

If this book had been written thirty years ago, the Communist states would no doubt have been held up as secular political orders just as significant as France or America. With the advantage of hindsight, however, we see them as the mirror image of theocracies (see Figure 4). In Marxist states, whether nominally secular or officially atheist, negligible protection of freedom of religion or belief is combined with active state promotion of orthodoxy in belief, identity, and practice. By 'establishing' a variety of atheism as the ideology of the state, promoting it because

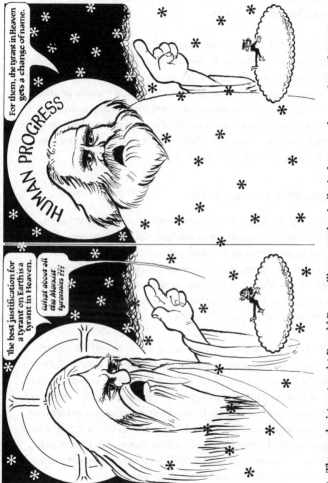

4. The secularist cartoonist Donald Rooum illustrates the similarity between theocracies and Marxist 'secularism'.

it is thought true and beneficent for human progress, and denying freedom and equality to the religious or those adopting different non-religious world views, these states satisfy none of the conditions for secularism.

Today only North Korea offers so extreme an example as Albania, torturing and enslaving dissidents and religious people (and doesn't dare be honest to the rest of the world about it). Officially secular, China also comes close to the establishment of materialist atheism. Although its constitution promises freedom of religion, in practice religions are subject to a number of severe state controls, and the atheism of the Communist Party is preferred over religions and over other non-religious world views.

Romantic conservatism

You do not have to be a theocrat or totalitarian atheist to deny the fairness argument for secularism. Not everyone sees the relationship between the state and its citizens as a rational social contract. For some, the nation commands loyalty on grounds of heritage and ethnicity. They argue each person is rooted in a particular society and tradition and is bound to their fellow members of that society by culture.

The politician and writer Edmund Burke (1729–97) was horrified by the innovations of the French Revolution. In 1790 in *Reflections on the Revolution in France* he set out his counter-revolutionary view that society was a sort of family that acquired its character by the inheritance of tradition: an organic system not a rational one. He had supported the American Revolution, seeing it as a natural development of traditions of English liberty, but he rejected France's rupture with its own heritage for the same reasons. Burke saw the individual constitution of any state as:

> but a clause in the great primaeval contract of eternal society,
> linking the lower with the higher natures, connecting the visible

and invisible world, according to a fixed compact sanctioned by
the inviolable oath which holds all physical and all moral natures,
each in their appointed place.

He was a strong supporter of establishment but, although he
described himself as a Christian, Burke was not a theocrat.
He believed that Hinduism was right for India and that Islam
was right for Arab lands. His primary concern was not for truth
but for national identity and social order. He said:

> When ancient opinions and rules of life are taken away, the loss
> cannot possibly be estimated. From that moment we have no compass
> to govern us; nor can we know distinctly to what port we steer … We
> know, and what is better, we feel inwardly, that religion is the basis
> of civil society, and the source of all good and of all comfort.

Over two centuries later, there is at least one French politician
who would be to Burke's liking. As president of the Republic of
France from 2007 to 2012, the conservative Nicolas Sarkozy
frequently expressed support for the idea of France as a Christian
society. Because of the deep-rooted attachment to the principle of
laïcité that exists in France, he went carefully and mostly confined
himself to arguing France should cultivate a secularism more
'open' to religion.

At the Vatican in 2007, Sarkozy questioned whether morality
divorced from religion could ever suffice and made a 'declaration
of repentance' because secularism 'cut France from its Christian
roots'. Secularism, he said, 'always risks exhausting itself or
transforming itself into fanaticism when it is not built against a
hope that fulfils the aspiration for the infinite'. In Riyadh in 2008,
in the heart of a totalitarian theocracy, he spoke of the
'transcendent God who is in the mind and heart of every man'.
Like Burke his was not a concern for truth—he expressed support
for the Islam of France's Arab population in the same terms as
he supported the Catholicism of the ethnic French.

Sarkozy's comments illustrate an important aspect of the romantic conservative case against secularism. Very often, it is built on a fear that, cut off from the traditional (religious) sources of its values and ethics, a society will become lawless and its members immoral. Religion is seen as a guarantor of civil culture and social morality and as an essential aspect of nationality. The same arguments have coloured recent statements by British Conservative politicians, by nationalist politicians in central and Eastern Europe, and by the regime of Putin in Russia which advocate a return to 'traditional values', but the argument is not just European.

The political campaigner and writer Vinayak Damodar Savarkar (1883–1966) was a sort of Indian Burke. He coined two terms that have become very important in Indian conservatism. *Hindutva* or 'Hinduness' is an ethnic identity meant to unite the people indigenous to the subcontinent of whatever religion or belief. *Hindu Rashtra* or 'Hindu political order' is nationalism based on this idea, which called for government to be built on native political traditions, not Western ones. Though an atheist himself, Savarkar defined a Hindu as 'He who considers India as both his Fatherland and Holyland' and said:

> we Hindus are bound together not only by the tie of the love we bear to a common fatherland and by the common blood that courses through our veins and keeps our hearts throbbing and our affections warm, but also by the tie of the common homage we pay to our great civilisation—our Hindu culture.

This attitude of romantic conservatism and ethnic nationalism has advocates today in many nations and on every continent. Secularists argue that it breeds prejudice and social exclusion of those with different beliefs and that it is unsustainable as a political ethic in diverse societies where it can never guarantee the peace that secularism may. But the conservatives are correct that any government does have to make moral choices in the course of its business. Is secularism undermined by this fact that governments can never be truly 'neutral'?

The myth of neutrality

The most sophisticated case against secularism comes not from its theocratic, nationalist, or conservative opponents but from liberal critics: its own children. Their argument strikes at the heart of secularism's most precious claims because they say that, far from guaranteeing the liberal freedoms it values, secularism inhibits their realization. Secularism pretends to be neutral, they say, but in separating religion from politics it is not neutral. It implicitly favours non-religious ways of reasoning, living, and thinking over religious ones. Even worse, because of its Western origins, the non-religious ways it privileges are those of a secularized Christianity—doubly incompatible with non-Christian religions. Today, when religious ways of living and thinking are still globally significant and perhaps resurgent, and when in Western countries there are growing numbers of followers of religions other than the Christianity of these countries' heritage, secularism is either redundant or needs serious modification.

The argument that secularism is not in fact objective is initially plausible. Proponents of secularism build their case on the claim that their way of organizing politics is an open framework that can appeal to all, including those of different religions. But it is plainly also an *alternative* to a political order founded on religion, and in most of its real-world occurrences it has been instituted in reaction to religious power. Many of its advocates at the times of its institution have been personally non-religious, from Jefferson to Atatürk to Nehru to the French revolutionaries.

What are the unshared assumptions that critics of secularism claim it carries? They point to the history of Europe that we examined in Chapter 2, pp. 8–18, and conclude that secularism is a consequence of a distinctively European religious and philosophical tradition. It was the religious warfare and strife of Europe that led to the development of toleration and a type of Christianity that was capable of being separated from the state. They say secularism relies on this theoretical and practical separation between 'the religious' and 'the secular' which is peculiar to the European Enlightenment and inapplicable to other parts of the world and other times. The main world views of modern Westerners—varieties of non-political Christianity, individual syncretic 'spiritualties', and a non-religious humanism—are well-fitted to secularism because they grew up together. Other types of world view from other cultures are not so fitted to secularism. The anthropologist Talal Asad argues that, although the Christian and Enlightenment heritage of their culture leads Westerners to see religion as a collection of personal beliefs, for others, it is something different, expressed primarily in public or community practice and essential to their identity and being. The assumption that religion can be separated from other areas of life and made private is, on this view, a Western imposition on the rest of the world.

Critics of secularism don't just argue that it depends on a particular and unshared view of religion. They also argue it depends on an unshared view of politics. They say that the idea that there is a difference between public and private is a product of Western political thought—or at least that secularists' idea of what is public is too large and impinges greatly on what others see as private. Western liberals may see schools as 'public' because the state provides them, but why could they not be seen as 'private' because they are where parents send their children?

These, so the argument runs, are the unshared assumptions of secularism. As a result, the secular state actively supports and privileges certain values and interests over others: individualism, for example, and the idea of religion as something negative to be contained. President Chirac of France, defending the banning of religious symbols in secular state schools, justified it because schools should be a 'sanctuary'. The implication is clear: the secular state protects individuals *against* religion. This has certainly been the case in France, where some feel that secularism seeks to homogenize society in a way that denies individuals the freedom of conscience that secularism should protect and demands more of Muslims than it demands of Catholics.

It certainly is the case that many non-Western anti-secularists do see secularism as undesirable because it is Western. In the course of a speech in 2014 denouncing freedom of conscience and of religion or belief, the prime minister of Malaysia denounced 'human rightism, where the core beliefs are based on humanism and secularism as well as liberalism' as a package of Western origin. In 1948 some Islamic states refused to adopt the Universal Declaration of Human Rights and in 1982 Iran's Ambassador to the UN said that it was a secularized version of the 'Judaeo-Christian tradition'. The liberal critics of secularism make common cause with such theocratic voices at least to the extent of agreeing that secularism is not 'neutral' but laden with values. With relative approval, they often point to Indian secularism as being more open and inclusive.

Liberal critics make a powerful case against a secularism that claims to be 'neutral', but this begs the question of whether any secularism does in fact so claim this, which is less obvious. Secularists rather argue that it is a value-laden political commitment that *may* be shared by people of different religions, not that it *is* in reality shared by everyone.

A community of communities

Many of those who advance the 'myth of neutrality' argument would rather see modern nations as collections of communities than as single societies. They argue that much of what makes life worth living comes from membership of a social group, and that such groups are the most important units of society. Those sharing religious identities are important examples of such groups and the role of the state and the law should be to treat these groups equally and protect them from interference. It is the group rather than the individual member of society that needs to be treated impartially by the state.

When instituted in practice, this can result in a radical multiculturalist policy. In its extreme version the approach is called 'pillarization' (originally a Dutch word: *verzuiling*). From the late 1800s, it was an important principle of political organization in both the Netherlands and Belgium. Instead of seeking to provide public institutions that would cater for all people in their common aspect as citizens, pillarization provided different institutions for different groups. In the Netherlands until the mid-20th century, Protestants, Catholics, Socialists, and Liberals/Freethinkers/Humanists each had their own separate schools, universities, hospitals, trade unions, political parties, and broadcasters. This strict division then began to dissolve, but vestiges remain in the provision of some public services.

Many European states formally register and regulate religious organizations and still more in practice pursue the same multiculturalist policy in some areas. In recent years, England has added Muslim, Sikh, and Hindu state schools to its existing Jewish and Christian ones, and parts of Germany have done the same. Nor is this approach confined to Europe. Indonesia was a colonial possession of the Netherlands and when independence came, there was strong pressure for an Islamic state to succeed the Dutch colonial one. Instead, the constitution of 1945 gave the state no religious designation but made general 'belief in one God' a constitutionally mandated part of national ideology. The state now officially recognizes six religions: Islam, Hinduism, Buddhism, Catholicism, Protestantism, and Confucianism. It maintains institutions for each of these denominations. There are many other such states and, as we've seen, India also exhibits some aspects of this multiculturalist approach within its secularism.

Secularist unease around all this focuses on the potential for conflict in the resulting social division and also on the rights of individuals. How can the rights of the individual to leave a group or to change identity be assured in such regimes? How can the rights of a dissident within a group be protected when the state has devolved many of its functions to the often highly conservative leaders of religious groups? And what about groups that are not recognized by the state, like atheists in Indonesia? In 2012 an Indonesian atheist Alexander Aan falsely said on an official form that he was a Muslim. He was imprisoned for this lie, but because Indonesia doesn't recognize non-religious people and give an option for that on official forms, he in fact could not have told the truth. In practice, pillarization can fossilize old divisions in society and limit the freedom of unrecognized minorities. Besides, although religion is important to some people, it is far from the only important aspect of someone's identity.

In examining some of the alternatives to secularism, we have come up against the reality that hardly any one of them is completely non-secular. Although pillarized states are entangled with religion, they are at least equidistant from the religions they acknowledge. Some of them, as some states with established churches do, attempt to secure freedom and equal treatment for all. In this sense they may be more secular than some states that formally separate themselves from religions. Bearing in mind all we have learned about states in the real world and the arguments over what is the best state–religion settlement, it is time to look again at the definition of secularism.

Chapter 6
Conceptions of secularism

We began this book with a definition of secularism based on the work of the French scholar Jean Baubérot:

- separation of religious institutions from the institutions of the state and no domination of the political sphere by religious institutions;

- freedom of thought, conscience, and religion for all, with everyone free to change their beliefs and manifest their beliefs within the limits of public order and the rights of others;

- no state discrimination against anyone on grounds of their religion or non-religious world view, with everyone receiving equal treatment on these grounds.

Our brief survey of the most notable secular states has confirmed that Baubérot's ideal secularism is not a political reality anywhere and never has been. Instead, we've uncovered a variety of configurations even in states that describe themselves officially as secular. They do not have identical laws, constitutions, or ways of relating to religious institutions. We've also seen that some states that are not officially secular are nonetheless in many ways secular in practice.

In fact debates continue to rage over the definition of 'secularism' between philosophers, sociologists, political scientists, campaigners, politicians, and lawyers, who all disagree with each other about what it should and should not mean.

Secularism and the secular

As we saw in Chapter 5, pp. 73–5, some question whether 'secularism' is a suitable term to describe political settlements outside the historically Christian West. Sociologists like Jose Casanova point out that the word presupposes the existence of the 'secular' separate from the 'religious' and that this assumption is Western, not universal. But although the words 'secular' and 'secularism' were coined in this cultural context, and the idea of secularism most fully articulated in it, the political situation in which religious life is distinguished from the life of the state is not unique to the West. They are very much a feature of it but they are also a feature of other places and times, and although their appearance in these places is in some instances conditioned by their encounter with ideas from European culture, it is not always so. In recent decades in particular, the experience of states like India refutes the suggestion that secularism is a solely Western phenomenon.

Nonetheless, Casanova's analysis is helpful in building a definition of secularism because it reminds us that, for many decades, secularism was indeed thought of as a Western phenomenon and today, when called 'secularism', is often rejected because of those associations, even by those whom we could call secularist in their views. In the broadest possible sense, secularism for Casanova is 'some principle of separation between religious and political authority'. This encourages us to think of secularism as being not just one thing, but as being a general approach of which there are many types. Such an acknowledgement of breadth helps us to sharpen up our examination of individual instances of secularism in different countries and ages without needing to meld them unnaturally into a single definition. We can admit there genuinely is something that state approaches to religions in Napoleonic

France, Revolutionary America, post-independence India, and Atatürk's republic have in common, even if they differ wildly at the next level down.

The Canadian academic Charles Taylor goes further than anyone in seeing secularism as originating as part and parcel of the European tradition and experience. Although he has contemplated it might be misleading to use a word with the connotations of 'secularism' to describe various settlements outside the West, he thinks in the end it makes sense to use the familiar word. This is a sensible decision. If we are mindful of the Christian and European origins of the word and remember that secularisms are in fact plural, it is still a useful term to describe at least a principle of distinction between religious authority or institutions and political authority and institutions. The vast majority of scholars agree and take this as their own starting point.

Two types of Western secularism

Certainly the dominant definition of secularism for many decades was that derived from the political experience of the West, but even within that 'secularism' there are at least two possible definitions. The US political scientist Elizabeth Shakman Hurd identifies these two types as 'Judeo-Christian secularism' and 'laicism'.

Laicism is anticlerical in character: state antipathy to religion forged in opposition to religious domination. Giving priority to the state and to common national identity over religion, it is focused on protecting citizens' freedom from religion as much as on guaranteeing freedom of religion.

Judaeo-Christian secularism by contrast draws inspiration from the theology that emphasizes freedom of conscience and from Enlightenment ideas of human dignity. This secularism is established to preserve the liberties of citizens to think, organize, and worship (or not) as they wish. It's a more internally contested, messier sort of secularism than laicism, partly due to its ambiguous parentage, partly because it defines itself by an absence (the lack of an establishment; the lack of confessional coercion) rather than being aligned with a positive national identity. It's an implicit rather than an explicit secularism.

Although the exemplars of these two secularisms are France and the US, it is possible to match other national configurations to these two models. But these two secularisms no longer offer an exhaustive range of the possible definitions. We live now in a world full of nation states, each with different political situations, albeit shaped by each other. In defining contemporary secularism we need to take a global view.

Separation of church and state

This phrase, used by Jefferson in the US as we saw, has gone on to be definitive of secularism for many. With the replacement of 'church' with 'religion', it has provided a definition applicable outside Western contexts. The British sociologist and political theorist Tariq Modood echoes it in his own broad definition of secularism as:

> institutional arrangements such that religious authority and religious reasons for action and political authority and political reasons for action are distinguished; so, political authority does not rest on religious authority and the latter does not dominate political authority.

Many academics define secularism in this minimal way and not as fully as Baubérot, who includes within his definition additional state aims of both freedom and equality. Others, however, see separation of church and state as not just insufficient for a state to be called secular, but actually less essential to the definition of secularism than freedom and equality.

The twin tolerations

The American political scientist Alfred Stepan has argued that separation should no longer be seen as necessary for us to call a state secular. He suggests instead a model he calls the 'twin tolerations' as a better definition. The parties to this mutual toleration are the state and religious institutions. In his most recent restatement of his view, on the one hand:

> Religious institutions should not have constitutionally privileged prerogatives that allow them authoritatively to mandate public policy to democratically elected officials or effectively to deny critical freedoms to any citizens.

At the same time, the state should ensure:

> not only the complete right to worship but the freedom of religious individuals and groups to advance their values in civil society publicly and to sponsor organizations and movements in political society, as long as their public advancement of these beliefs does not impinge negatively on the liberties of other citizens or violate democracy and the law by violence or other means.

For Stepan, the important features of secularism are the securing of freedom of conscience and reduction of discrimination. If we take these as secularism's main features, he claims his analysis better describes the situation that secures those benefits than a model based on an ideal *laïcité*. He argues we should accept there are 'multiple secularisms' in addition to those of the US and France, and to this widened definition of secularisms he admits not only states like India but even states with single established churches like Norway and Denmark and states that officially recognize a number of denominations like the Netherlands and Belgium.

Stepan denies it makes sense to exclude states like these, which are not in thrall to overweening religious establishments and have high levels of freedom of conscience, from our conception of secularism at the same time as we are willing to describe a state like Turkey, with its severe limitations on freedom, as secular. Part of his agenda is to disentangle the definition of democracy from secularism in the interests of spreading the former in regions where secularism is unlikely to appeal. As he puts it:

> The word 'secularism' carries a lot of negative baggage in Arab countries because for many speakers of Arabic the word has a connotation that is anti-religious. So if the argument is 'Democracy must be secular,' and if people are parsing that in their heads in an Arabic speaking country, they may be understandably putting some version of the following question to themselves: 'If secularism means being anti-religious, and if to be a democracy you must be secular, then as a good Muslim should I support democracy?'

The idea of 'twin tolerations' is useful in prompting us to think about what the most crucial constituents of secularism really are. It also allows us to separate the question of whether a state is secular or not from the fact that it may call itself secular. Norway does not call itself a secular state, whereas Turkey does. Stepan would say that in fact Turkey has a far weaker claim to be secular in practice than Norway, and the model of the twin tolerations provides a framework for demonstrating and justifying this claim. It also reminds us that secularism is not necessary for democracy but may be a feature of non-democratic states and it gives us a way of dividing secularisms—the democratic from the non-democratic—which is useful in a detailed definition.

But although his theory is one of *twin* tolerations, Stepan gives comparatively little attention to religious institutions and hierarchs. In his definition of secularism, this leads to a downplaying of the importance of the freedom of the individual *from* religion. In this vein, it is not clear why Stepan wants to call state church or pillarized systems 'secular'. Why does he not just say that many church–state arrangements can be conducive to freedom of conscience and the necessary political distance to make a polity free and democratic? Indonesia and Belgium discriminate against those not in the favoured group of religions. Can we really call a state secular that prefers some religions over others in this way?

Principled distance

If the secularisms exemplified in the West are no longer sufficient to describe all secularisms, perhaps it is to India we should turn to augment our definition. The Indian political theorist Rajeev Bhargava thinks so. He agrees that an over-reliance on Western theoretical and ideological definitions has brought secularism to the dangerous position where some non-Westerners reject it and that it needs redefinition. Unlike Stepan, however, Bhargava rejects the claim that any state with an official religion could be deemed secular.

For Bhargava, state institutions must be constitutionally separated from religious institutions to guarantee the formal equality of citizenship that is essential for a secular state. But he would allow state and religion to work together and the state to intervene in religions. Taking India as his example, Bhargava does not see secularism as meaning the privatizing of religion or the maximizing of religious freedom. He sees it instead as a necessary principle of statecraft in the context of social diversity. In such contexts the state needs actively to avoid any one group dominating another and causing harms from social marginalization through to active state oppression. Secularism is the way they do this.

Denying the desirability of strict and total separation, Bhargava promotes the idea of 'principled distance' as the definition that should govern the state's involvement. The idea has two parts. First, the state doesn't have to have strict rules about impartially never intervening or always intervening in religions—instead, these decisions can be made in context. The state may or may not engage depending on the facts of the situation and the religion. If a religion's involvement promotes values integral to the state's secularism, such as human rights or sex equality, that involvement is permitted. The state is also allowed to intervene in religions to promote those same values. We saw examples of this in practice in India, where the state once intervened to eliminate some religion-based caste discrimination. Second, the state may treat people or groups differently in order to treat individuals as equals. A good example of this is the way that safety laws in the UK exempt Sikhs from the otherwise legal requirement to wear motorcycle helmets. The state does not have to behave in the same way to all: 'All it must ensure is that the relationship between the state and religions is guided by non-sectarian motives consistent with some values and principles.'

Bhargava's secular state can intervene in order to secure religious freedom for minorities, to minimize and eliminate instances of oppression, discrimination, and marginalization of one group by another, and to promote other secular policy ends such as gender and social equality. A major weakness in 'principled distance', however, is the question of what principles ought to inform it and how their application is to be policed. The particular historical situation of India conditioned the Indian answer to this question, but can the values of secularism really be as contingent as that?

Or is it perhaps an advantage in Bhargava's definition that the starting point for it is the plural society of India? As societies in the West that were more uniform become more heterogeneous, definitions from India may be useful in establishing a modern conception of secularism. Bhargava sees political and citizenship rights as areas where the state should be blind to religion but other areas of law and policy as being open to principled distance.

His partiality for secularism is pragmatic: it is better than the alternatives of domination by any one group. He agrees with Stepan that the formal establishment of Denmark is better than the confessional states of Saudi Arabia or Pakistan, and that the multiple establishments of Belgium or the Netherlands are better than the single establishment of Denmark, but he doesn't think either of them is as good as the secularism of India or the US.

This definition calls our attention to the fact that a state that is formally secular has its own aims, which are different from the aims of the religions. Bhargava recognizes there can be conflict between the two and he accepts that the state acting in pursuit of its aims is not 'neutral'. It is just that its aims are not mixed up with religious ones. His secularism is capable of the dynamism that a modern political doctrine must surely be capable of in a fast-changing world. As he says, it 'forever requires fresh interpretations, contextual judgements, and attempts at reconciliation and compromise'; as such it cuts through some of the liberal criticisms of secularism.

Secularism as a shared political ethic

Even states with non-secular constitutions like the UK, Denmark, or Norway have, as we saw, developed a secularism in practice: a way of speaking about and debating political questions that tries to be outside and above religious considerations in order to be in principle inclusive of all citizens' participation.

This secularism means everybody trying to speak in a shared language in the political sphere. In *Political Liberalism*, in 1993, John Rawls said this required us all to 'take the truths of religion off the political agenda'. If not they would disrupt a public space that ought to be accessible to all and cause unnecessary and irrelevant conflict. This view is not uncontroversial. Charles Taylor does not see why religious values in particular should be specifically excluded from public debate, given that they are by no means the only values that make appeals to concepts that are unshared. Why should religious people be disadvantaged, as he sees it, as against non-religious people? Nonetheless, this definition of secularism as a democratic practice is endorsed not just by academics but by practical politicians such as US President Barack Obama, who affirmed: 'the religiously motivated must translate their concerns into universal, rather than religion-specific values. Their proposals must be subject to argument and reason, and should not be accorded any undue automatic respect.'

The universal values Obama speaks of constitute what Rawls called 'overlapping consensus', which can bring citizens together in practice in a way that unshared religions or non-religious world views never can.

Proliferating secularisms

The British theologian Rowan Williams has distinguished between Rawls's 'programmatic secularism', which wants to deny religious arguments in the public sphere, and 'procedural secularism' which would admit such arguments but not necessarily privilege them. He prefers the latter secularism and says it is more democratic. At the theoretical level, academics often divide secularism into types in order to prefer one to the other in ways that connect with the definitions we have explored. Charles Taylor has distinguished between 'open' and 'closed' secularism to distinguish between a secularism that will make accommodations for the practices of religious citizens, which he supports, and a secularism that is hostile to religion. Tariq Modood has distinguished between the 'radical secularism' embodied by separation as in the US or France and 'moderate secularism', which describes the ethic of European liberal democracies he views as evolved and pragmatic. Modood sees 'moderate secularism' as maintaining the 'mutual autonomy' of religion and state but allowing the state to get involved in 'bringing out the public good element of organized religion (and not just protecting the public good from the dangers that organized religion can pose)'.

Today's academics strive for consensus as little as the philosophers of the Enlightenment; so theoretical secularism remains something of which there are and will continue to be many types.

Secularism in constitutions

The Comparative Constitutions Project at the University of Texas at Austin in the US has documented and assembled the constitutions of nearly every independent state in the world. Constitutions change from time to time but an analysis of the project's database in 2016 showed that over seventy of the 195 constitutions declare a separation of religion from the state. Some do this by simply describing the state as 'secular'; some declare separation of religion and state; some prohibit the establishment of any religion; some do all of these. Only around thirty states make a declaration to the effect that the state has an official religion. In addition, most states' constitutions provide for at least one aspect of secularism: over 180 of them guarantee freedom of religion or belief.

Of the states that describe themselves as 'secular', many are following France in doing so, having had a Francophone history. Most simply assert the secular nature of the state; some (especially those from Francophone postcolonial states) intertwine that status, as the constitution of France does, with democracy, the rule of law, and equality before the law. So, in the French constitution's preamble, we see: 'France shall be an indivisible, secular, democratic and social Republic. It shall ensure the equality of all citizens before the law, without distinction of origin, race or religion.' The constitution of Gabon, which was a colony of France until 1960, declares: 'Gabon is an indivisible, secular, democratic and social Republic.'

The states that don't describe themselves as secular but do declare separation differ as to their emphasis but convey the same general meaning. The 'first amendment' to the US constitution, as we have seen, declares: 'Congress shall make no law respecting an establishment of religion.' Bolivia's constitution declares: 'The State is independent of religion.' Portugal's states: 'Churches and other religious communities shall be separate from the state.' Paraguay's declares: 'No religious faith will have official character.' Some states have additional provisions that specifically declare the secular nature of state education. 'Education in Nicaragua is secular,' says its constitution, and Ecuador, Mexico, and many other states make the same provision.

In the case of constitutional guarantees of freedom of religion or belief, the devil is in the detail. A small minority of them are simple declarations along the lines of Bolivia's 'The State respects and guarantees freedom of religion and spiritual beliefs, according to their view of the world,' or South Korea's 'All citizens shall enjoy freedom of religion.' Others are detailed, specifying and in some cases thereby limiting in various ways the freedom of religion or belief to be enjoyed. As we saw in Chapter 3, pp. 44–5, many of these clauses from the mid-20th century onwards are modelled on international standards derived from the 1948 Universal Declaration of Human Rights. After the Declaration emphasis was given internationally to the constitutional protection of human rights, and many states incorporated the right to freedom of religion or belief into their national fundamental law. Adopting standard words for convenience or conforming to an international norm for the sake of credibility explains these off-the-peg clauses, which are seldom accompanied by a more detailed definition of secularism.

Although the secularism we find in constitutions is diverse, it could broadly fall into two types in the way that Shakman Hurd suggests. There is the *laïcité* of the French tradition, most obvious in Francophone former colonies and in parts of Latin America, and the freedom of religion of the US tradition in nations like Australia, where we find:

> The Commonwealth shall not make any law for establishing any religion, or for imposing any religious observance, or for prohibiting the free exercise of any religion, and no religious test shall be required as a qualification for any office or public trust under the Commonwealth.

Beyond this, there is no one constitutional definition of secularism, but the most recently adopted—that of Fiji, from 2013—at least gives an up-to-date example. It is a comprehensive assertion of all the aspects of secularism prescribed by Baubérot and more.

Box 2 Section 4 of the constitution of Fiji

4. SECULAR STATE

1. Religious liberty, as recognised in the Bill of Rights, is a founding principle of the State.
2. Religious belief is personal.
3. Religion and the State are separate, which means-
   a. the State and all persons holding public office must treat all religions equally;
   b. the State and all persons holding public office must not dictate any religious belief;
   c. the State and all persons holding public office must not prefer or advance, by any means, any particular religion, religious denomination, religious belief, or religious practice over another, or over any non-religious belief; and
   d. no person shall assert any religious belief as a legal reason to disregard this Constitution or any other law.

Campaigning secularists

Away from the theories of academics and the law of constitutions, there is the secularism advanced by its advocates in politics and civil society. This secularism is explicitly an ideal, an ideal towards which its proponents wish their national—and international—politics to strive.

The UK has the longest established campaigns for secularism that have not yet achieved their aims. There, Humanists UK defines secularism as 'the principle that, in a plural, open society where people follow many different religious and non-religious ways of life, the communal institutions that we share (and together pay for) should provide a neutral public space where we can all meet on equal terms' and promotes it as 'the best strategy for achieving freedom, equality, and peace in a plural society'. The organization British Muslims for Secular Democracy emphasizes the role of secularism in promoting a 'harmonious' society and says secular democracy offers 'a shared vision of citizenship' and 'the separation of faith and state, so faiths exert no undue influence on policies and there is a shared public space'. The National Secular Society says that secularism 'involves two basic propositions. The first is the strict separation of the state from religious institutions. The second is that people of different religions and beliefs are equal before the law.' It says secularism is 'the best chance we have to create a society in which people of all religions or none can live together fairly and peacefully'. It also has a more detailed ten-point manifesto for a secular state which, though in part reflecting its origins in the UK, sketches out a universal secularism that most of secularism's contemporary advocates could rally to.

Campaigning secularists would obviously warm most to Baubérot's definition of secularism, and indeed, if we are still seeking one ideal type of secularism to which we can judge states as approaching more or less closely, his definition holds up well.

Applied to states, it may sometimes yield difficult conclusions—a state like Turkey, which declares itself secular at the constitutional level and has been seen by many as paradigmatically so, may be found to be less secular in practice than a constitutionally Christian state like the UK. But Baubérot's three ingredients of secularism—freedom of religion or belief, equal treatment, the separation of religious and state authorities—do reflect at least the aspiration of many secularizing states and offer a fuller account of what real secularists aim for today than a simple definition of secularism as separation of church and state.

Still, in reality there are many secularisms. There are the secularisms of the campaigners and idealists, who differ according to their time and place. There are the secularisms of constitutions, specific efforts at one moment to crystallize these principles into the provisions of law, sometimes the result of earnest idealism, sometimes of political necessity or crisis, sometimes of lip service to an international norm. There are the secularisms of the practical politicians, struggling to find a way to persuade and govern in the real world. Then there are the secularisms of the academics, working to analyse the real world of politics and—just as often—to generate their own ideals. All these conceptions of secularism influence each other, and all have their partisans and their critics. Today they are more contentious than ever as, in the early 21st century, unresolved questions of long standing and new conflicts of great intensity are assailing secularism from every direction.

Chapter 7
Hard questions and new conflicts

Secularism has always been controversial. But today both the official secularism of constitutional republics and the secular ethic of liberal democracies are also being rocked by rapid social changes, resurgent religious identities and nationalisms, increasing migration, and many other factors. Secularism is an idea under siege by its opponents at the same time as conflicts within secularism pit its different aspects against each other in new tensions.

Secularism in practice

Jonathan Fox coordinates the Religion and State Project at Bar-Ilan University in Israel. It aims to describe, categorize, and analyse the approaches to religion of states worldwide and has done so for 177 countries. Rather than look simply at constitutions, it examines laws, regulations, government policies, and government actions in the various states to identify the general 'policy' of a country to religion. From his analysis Fox has created fourteen subcategories grouped into four bigger categories above them (see Table 1).

States in category 1 range from fully religious states like Saudi Arabia and Iran to the United Kingdom and Malta, which

Table 1. Fox's four categories of religion–state arrangements

Category	State...	Number of states
1	...has an official religion.	41
2	...supports a preferred religion or religions without declaring an official religion.	77
3	...treats religions neutrally.	43
4	...is hostile to religions.	16

privilege but don't enforce one particular religion and don't themselves dominate that religion's activities.

States in category 2 are equally diverse, giving preferential treatment to one or a number of religions with fine grades of distinction. There are states like Thailand, which privileges Buddhism but also Islam and Christianity on a level below that; Austria, which divides religions into types and privileges them in grades according to size and age; Belgium, which recognizes a number of religious and non-religious groups and privileges them equally in contrast to all others. Privileges vary but include things like tax exemptions, the right to run state schools or teach lessons in state-run schools, salaries at state expense, or the provision of buildings. Into this category, Fox puts the secularism of India.

States in category 3—'neutral' states—are divided into those that support all religions equally (typically at a very low level, like Nepal or New Zealand) and those that give no significant support to any religions, but do not do so out of hostility. Into this category Fox places the secularism of the US.

States in category 4 are ones that Fox judges to be hostile to religions. They express their hostility in one of two ways: either separation or control. Separationist states may support or fund religion at some nugatory level but they also regulate it heavily and seek to confine it to the private sphere of life. Into this category Fox places the *laïcité* of modern France. Perhaps surprisingly, given what we have seen of its practical workings, he puts the *laiklik* of Turkey in this same subcategory. Controlling countries are those like Vietnam, Kyrgyzstan, and China, where the state sets up official religious institutions that it uses to 'contain' religiosity.

We already know how few states declare themselves 'secular' in their constitutions, but Fox's analysis raises the question of whether we can claim the existence of any coherent and consistent real-world secularism at all. In his most recent analysis of his data from 2008, published in 2015, he shows that even official constitutional secularism rarely, if ever, means that the state is 'secular' in a way that would meet even one aspect of Baubérot's definition. There are states that officially declare themselves as 'secular' or as having separation of church and state in the second, third, and fourth of Fox's categories. The states that we have examined in this book as archetypically secular are spread across the categories. More than that, there are states in Fox's first category (Malta, for example) that are more secular in practice than states that are officially secular and are in his third category (Senegal, for example).

Fox argues that, if secularism is taken as meaning neutrality or separation, then only a maximum of 40 per cent of states that declare themselves secular could be generously analysed as being so in practice in 2008. Only thirteen states in 2008 had almost no involvement with religions: Taiwan, Japan, and South Korea in Asia; Benin, Burkina Faso, Congo, Namibia, and South Africa in Africa; Ecuador, Guyana, Uruguay, and the US in the Americas; and Estonia in Europe. It gets worse. We saw in Chapter 6, pp. 88–9, that 90 per cent of states guarantee freedom of religion or belief in their fundamental law, but Fox points outs that over 80 per cent of these states nonetheless restrict minority religions in ways they don't restrict the dominant religion. Almost no states provide equal treatment in practice. According to Fox there are fifty-one ways in which states support the religions or world views they favour, twenty-nine ways in which they restrict the religions or world views they favour, and thirty ways in which states restrict minority religions or world views. All of these are common in many states.

What all this illustrates is the precarious nature of secularism as a meaningful category in today's world, but Fox's analysis demonstrates an even greater challenge for secularism. His latest data are from 2008, but he can compare the situation then with the situation back to 1990. Over this period, many states changed their policy in small ways but twenty-one states made sufficiently large changes that Fox moved them from one category to another. Only six—Sweden, Nepal, Paraguay, Sudan, Iraq, and Portugal—moved in a more secular direction. More than twice as many—fifteen—increased their support for one or more religions.

If there is such a thing as a global tendency in religion–state relations today, it is in the opposite direction from the secular.

Schools and education

Controversy related to education has been a feature of secularism since the beginning. Historically, official secularism coincided with the construction of state school systems, when education moved from being the preserve of parents and informal communities (often religious) to being the concern of a class of trained specialists funded by the public. Campaigning secularists from the late 18th century onwards developed manifestos for a secular education system, and in some states this has been achieved at least in part. Their state schools are open to all children without prejudice and have curricula free from confessional religious instruction or practice. In many more states, however, religious institutions have significant involvement in the state education system: running schools, writing the curriculum, sending religious officials into schools as educators, inspecting schools, and in other ways. In almost every country in the world today, state education is a major arena for conflict between secularists and anti-secularists and between secularists with different approaches.

One clear principle of secularism is that there should be no domination of state institutions by religious institutions. It is very obvious, then, that the state systems of countries like Iran or Ireland, where schools are overwhelmingly dominated by one particular religion, are not secular. Here the curriculum is a tool of religious instruction, whatever else it may be, and one particular favoured religious organization has active involvement in the life and structure of the state's schools.

But what if *all* religious organizations are given the same participation in state schools as each other? If *all* religious organizations are allowed to run separate confessional classes in state schools, as they do in Belgium, or run separate state schools, as in England, wouldn't this equal treatment be consistent with secularism? To make it fair, provision could be made in proportion to their followers or in proportion to the number of parents that followed each religion. No one religion would be dominating the state institutions unfairly and everyone would be treated equally without discrimination. Wouldn't this satisfy the majority of the conditions of secularism as a result?

The first obvious objection is that many parents have non-religious world views (in some societies, most parents) and so the system would still be unfair, but perhaps we could take care of that. Humanist organizations could also be involved to cater for the non-religious, as they are in the Netherlands and parts of Germany. In these countries, as in Belgium, there are secularists who would defend such a system. But even if we could take care of the non-religious within a comprehensive system and so

guarantee fairness to these parents, there are good reasons to
think that such a system would still not end up being compatible
with secularism.

The first reason is that such a system in the real world does not
allow for changing patterns of belief and affiliation. In the nature
of things it cannot react promptly to such changes and so over
time privileges those religions or beliefs that are strong at the time
the system is initiated. It provides them with recognition and
resources and protects them from the effects of loss of popularity
while making it difficult for new religions or world views to
grow and gain recognition, inhibiting freedom of belief and
equal treatment.

Second, no state would be able to run such a system fairly. There
are so many denominations of Christianity alone that providing a
whole school (or even a regular separate class in a shared school)
for every one of them in every place would be impossible. Even
more challenging, although people often think of religions as
homogeneous ('Catholics think this'; 'Buddhists think that'), the
reality is that individuals are not so consistent. One person may
identify as a Catholic but believe in reincarnation and not think
that contraception is sinful. She may be married to someone
who identifies as a Muslim but sympathizes in some of his beliefs
with some aspects of pantheism and at home keeps Christmas
because of his own mixed parentage and upbringing. Belief,
identity, and practice are so individual that to provide a school
that catered for each parental situation without discrimination
would be impossible.

Third, is it even right to focus solely on parents? We saw when
we were discussing the case for secularism in Chapter 4 that the
'fairness' argument applies not just to adults but to children too.
The right of children to freedom of religion or belief (at least in
line with their developing capacity) would suggest at a minimum
that the education system provided by the state should be one free

of religious assumptions on contested questions like the basis of morality or the purpose of life and certainly that it should not enforce religious practices. Going even further, if state secularism really seeks to protect freedom of conscience, we could also argue that the state system should equip children with the skills and experience and ability to choose. The secular state school should teach about religions and non-religious world views in an objective, fair, and balanced way, allowing no confessional instruction and actively seeking to equip children with the critical skills needed to make up their own minds.

This is the thinking behind the *Convention on the Rights of the Child*, adopted by the United Nations General Assembly in 1989, Article 13 of which declares:

> The child shall have the right to freedom of expression; this right shall include freedom to seek, receive and impart information and ideas of all kinds, regardless of frontiers, either orally, in writing or in print, in the form of art, or through any other media of the child's choice.

Article 14 of the Convention says that states 'shall respect the right of the child to freedom of thought, conscience, and religion' and that parents can 'provide direction to the child in the exercise of his or her right in a manner consistent with the evolving capacities of the child', but it does not say that the state has an obligation to provide this on the parents' behalf.

So we come to the interests of the state itself. Secularism accepts that individual freedom of religion or belief may be limited to protect the rights of others or in the interests of public order. The state's interest in social cohesion and equal citizenship may come into play here, in line with the pragmatic argument for secularism rehearsed in Chapter 4, pp. 54–5. The state can be argued to have a legitimate interest in ensuring that children who will be citizens together learn with and from each other from an early age to develop the skills and habits of living together in a democratic society. A Balkanized system would hardly achieve that.

So, although the argument from fairness might to some extent support the case for every denomination to have its own quota of religious schools in the public system in proportion to its strength in the society at large, the arguments for freedom and peace provide a case against.

Blasphemy and criticism of religions

Along with education, the question of free expression looms large in some of the fiercest debates and most violent confrontations over secularism today.

In non-secular states, speech and expression are routinely regulated. In Christian Europe various laws curtailed and punished—even with death—not only blasphemy and insults against the established religion but even heretical and dissenting disagreement with it, just as they do today in Islamic states from Iran to Pakistan. In contrast, freedom of expression was a fundamental value to the Enlightenment thinkers who gave full shape to Western secularism. The same amendment to the US constitution in the 18th century that guaranteed the free exercise of religion also guaranteed freedom of speech. In our own time, the abolition of antique laws against 'blasphemy' has been hailed in those countries where it has occurred only recently (for example, in England and Wales in 2008 or in Iceland in 2015) as a milestone on the route to a more secular state. In India there are many secularists who share this view and wish to abolish laws that curb free expression by criminalizing religious insults and the incitement of hatred on religious grounds. But there are also secularists who defend some such limitation of expression on religious matters so as to ensure peace and avoid heightened tensions and inter-communal violence. In Western democracies with increasingly religiously diverse societies, the case is being pressed that there too it may be right to limit speech in the interests of peace—and that to do so would not be anti-secularist. Talal Asad has argued that some prohibition of certain forms of speech should be deemed compatible with secularism. He argues that the deliberate violation of what is ardently believed by many Muslims to be prohibitions within Islam, such as the depiction of its founder, is a form of aggression against Muslims and could be legitimately curtailed. Such restrictions may perhaps be prudential but they are not easily compatible with secularism for long; admitting any restrictions risks opening a Pandora's box of competing claims of offence and demands.

In the West, the case which galvanized both the opponents and supporters of free expression about religion was undoubtedly the furore which greeted the publication in 1988 of *The Satanic Verses* by the British Indian novelist Sir Salman Rushdie. The use within the novel of themes and characters related to Islam made it offensive to some Muslims, who considered it sacrilegious. Thousands of British Muslims in the town of Bolton and the city of Bradford held public demonstrations in which they burnt the book (see Figure 5). Within months it had been banned in India, Bangladesh, Sudan, Sri Lanka, South Africa, Kenya, Thailand, Tanzania, Indonesia, and Singapore. Dozens of booksellers in the US and UK were firebombed or threatened with violence. Potent symbolism was in play on both sides. For the Muslims who were offended, Rushdie had committed an unpardonable crime in mocking sacred figures. For the liberals who condemned the reactions, the burning of books recalled the censorious destruction of literature by the fascists of Nazi Germany, who lit bonfires of banned books in the 1930s. Their feeling was of violence being done against secular principles and freedoms. The affair escalated into an international diplomatic situation when a demonstration of thousands in Pakistan against an American cultural centre led to several protestors being killed. Ayatollah Khomeini of Iran issued a death sentence against Rushdie under Islamic law and called for any Muslim who got the chance to kill him. For many

5. British Muslims burning *The Satanic Verses* in 1989.

years, Rushdie lived in hiding under police protection and even now the sentence has not been revoked. Indeed, Iranian state media declared it renewed in 2016.

At the time of the Rushdie affair, the archbishop of Canterbury, Robert Runcie, called for the English law criminalizing blasphemy to be extended to religions other than Anglican Christianity. The UK government responded immediately to say they would not consider this, and an attempted private prosecution of Rushdie, which would have extended the blasphemy law to Islam, ended in failure. Nonetheless, both in the UK and elsewhere in the world, the calls of religious groups for laws to prevent the insulting of religion escalated in subsequent years.

Cartoons of the character of Mohammed have sparked the most serious recent escalation of the conflict in Europe between those who uphold the secularist value of free expression on religious matters and those who seek to enforce blasphemy norms. In 2005, the Danish newspaper *Jyllands-Posten* published cartoons of

Mohammed as a way of commenting on self-censorship in Denmark. An editorial accompanying the cartoons explained that this recent tendency was:

> incompatible with contemporary democracy and freedom of speech, where one must be ready to put up with insults, mockery, and ridicule...we are on our way to a slippery slope where no-one can tell how the self-censorship will end.

In many states with majority Muslim populations there was a violent reaction and trade bans on Danish goods. In the West some called for moderation and for needless offence not to be caused; others called for the tradition of free speech not to be broken in the face of new censors. One French magazine in particular heeded this latter call. Secularist and socialist, *Charlie Hebdo* is a satirical magazine with its origins in the 1960s and with a particular fondness for cartoons, especially of religious or other authority figures. Banned at one point by the French government for political satire, the magazine gained a reputation for opposition to censorship of all kinds. In response to the controversy around the *Jyllands-Posten* cartoons, *Charlie Hebdo* reprinted them and commissioned some additional cartoons too. For the next decade, they published a number of cartoons of Mohammed.

On 7 January 2015, two French Muslims of Algerian descent broke into the offices of *Charlie Hebdo* and shot dead twelve staff, shouting in Arabic that God was great and that the prophet had been avenged. There was a great outpouring of popular support for the magazine in the following days and weeks. The French government donated a million euros for its continued publication; many thousands took to the streets in France and elsewhere to show solidarity with its values.

But in a way, violence and the threat of violence triumphed. Decision makers in many Western media outlets refused to show the cartoons that offended the killers, either because they did not wish to cause offence themselves or out of fear for their own lives or those of their staff. Even without the force of law, the threat of violence enforced religious taboos in secular states no less than elsewhere.

This attempt to impose religious laws and taboos on people unconnected with the religion is now a global phenomenon. Internationally, pressure to outlaw not just blasphemy but even criticism of religions has been spearheaded by the Organization of Islamic Cooperation (OIC), a coalition of countries with Muslim populations, which for many years sponsored successful resolutions in the United Nations to this effect, until the Western democracies, under pressure from secularist campaigners, organized sufficient opposition to defeat them. The OIC has not renounced its ambition to see religions protected from criticism and continues to promote the idea and defend it on grounds of religious freedom. In the early 21st century, Islamic states are wealthier and hence more influential globally than in the 20th century, and less likely to pay lip service to secular norms. They find support from the autocratic regime in Russia and the domestically repressive state of China, which do not prize freedom of expression or of belief, and they may yet succeed in their aims.

Muslim advocates of restrictions are in the vanguard, but they are not alone. In 2004 in the UK, Sikh protestors successfully intimidated the Birmingham Repertory Theatre into cancelling performances of *Behzti*, a play by a Sikh playwright that they said offended their religion. Hindu extremists in the West have campaigned against Hindu gods and goddesses being depicted on shoes, skateboards, and other merchandise. Their claims of offence have often been successful, with online retailer Amazon removing clothing depicting Hindu deities from sale in 2014 and doormats in 2016 and online retailer Alibaba doing the same in 2016 with a range of yoga mats.

Religious expression in a secular state: religious dress and symbols

Free expression about religion is the cause of one set of controversies, but equally controversial has been free expression of religion. Here, it is not just words and pictures in dispute, but other forms of personal expression and their place in a secular state.

In 1989 three girls were suspended from their state school in northern France because they refused to remove their headscarves, which they said they wore as a religious obligation. In a France where, as we saw in Chapter 2, pp. 22–3, the religious appeared to have come to terms with secularism, this event was a cultural shock. The French mainstream saw schools as spaces belonging to the republic and any religious display within them as therefore offensive to *laïcité*. The event kick-started what became known as *l'affaire du foulard* ('the affair of the scarf') and, within fourteen years, had led to the banning of all ostentatious religious symbols from public schools.

Initially, it was not clear that the situation would end in a ban. The Council of State, France's highest legal authority, advised that the wearing of the headscarf was in principle compatible with secularism. The Council said:

> the wearing by students of symbols by which they intend to manifest their religious affiliation is not by itself incompatible with the principle of secularism, as it constitutes the free exercise of freedom of expression and of manifestation of religious creeds.

For any ban to be legal, it would have to be demonstrated that it only affected:

> signs of religious affiliation that, due to their nature, or the conditions in which they are worn individually or collectively, or

due to their ostentatious and provocative character, would constitute an act of pressure, provocation, proselytism or propaganda, or would harm the dignity or the freedom of the student or other members of the educative community, or would compromise their health or safety, or would perturb the educational activities or the education role of the teaching personnel, or would trouble public order in the establishment or the normal functioning of the public service.

France's socialist education minister issued guidance that it was up to schools on a case-by-case basis whether they wished to allow it or not. But just one month later, three more girls were expelled from their school, and over the coming years the situation escalated, with teachers in the east of France going on strike against the wearing of the headscarf in schools and more girls being expelled. In 1994, the new education minister, from the political left but further to the right than his predecessor and a strongly committed secularist (though also a devout Roman Catholic), issued guidance that said that although discreet religious symbols were compatible with the secularism of state schools, more visible symbols like the headscarf were not. In the next decade, over a hundred girls were expelled from schools for wearing it, though many had their expulsions reversed by the courts, which continued to make case-by-case decisions in a way that increased public pressure—especially pressure from professional educators—for clear rules one way or another.

Muddling through was not working. In 2003, President Jacques Chirac established a commission chaired by Bernard Stasi, the government ombudsman, to report on the best modern application of secularism as established in the 1905 law. The commission reported within the year. It affirmed that 'Freedom of conscience, equal rights, and the neutrality of the political power' should be afforded to everyone and found that in recent years the social contract in France had been 'undermined', the situation of women and girls had been worsening, and divisive community identities had been increasing. In light of this, it affirmed a policy of strict secularism in relation to religious symbols in public institutions like the school. However, the commission also recommended a policy of 'reasonable accommodation' in other areas, such as in public school canteens, where it recommended that religious dietary requirements be met, and in the declaring of public holidays, suggesting that Jewish and Muslim holidays should be included alongside Christian ones.

In his response to the report, President Chirac called on all citizens to unite around 'our common values of respect, tolerance, dialogue' and decided that a new law was needed. In 2004 the law 'concerning, as an application of the principle of the separation of church and state, the wearing of symbols or garb which show religious affiliation in public primary and secondary schools' was passed. It prohibited the wearing of conspicuous religious symbols such as headgear worn by Jews, Muslims, and Sikhs, but permitted less conspicuous religious symbols like jewellery, such as the crosses often worn by Christians. Other recommendations of the Stasi Commission, in favour of increased accommodation of religious minorities, were not implemented.

Controversy over visible religious symbols and their threat to public order has not ended there. In 2010, covering the face in public places was banned in France in a law that was targeted at Muslim women doing so for religious reasons. Only two members of the legislature voted against the ban on grounds of freedom, and, on appeal to the European Court of Human Rights, the ban was upheld on the novel grounds that it was legitimate for the state to defend certain social norms that allowed people to live better together as citizens. In 2016, the authorities in a number of seaside resort towns in France, beginning with the mayor of Villeneuve-Loubet on the Côte d'Azur, banned the wearing of 'burkinis' on their beaches. The burkini is an all-enveloping swimming costume marketed to Muslim women as a way of meeting religious obligations to cover your body in public. On this occasion, the Council of State upheld the right of religious women in a secular state to wear what they wished and made it clear that any ban was 'a serious and manifestly illegal attack on fundamental freedoms'. No threat to public order by Muslim women in burkinis had been proven and so no limitation of their rights was justified.

The case of religious symbols in France has parallels in other countries from the UK to Turkey and illustrates two challenges for secularism.

The first is a tension between the rights of those who want to manifest religious beliefs and the rights of others. The wearing of religious clothes and symbols in the course of your daily life is the freedom of every person guaranteed by secularism (see Figure 6). As we've seen, secularism will also allow this freedom to be limited if it can be shown to impinge on public order or the rights of others. Most people agree that this means there are some cases where religious clothing and symbols that impede the

6. French Muslims invoke the values of secularism to support practices many secularists oppose.

performance of duties in employment or other obligations can be forbidden. The wearing of crosses on long chains that may become entangled in machinery or may touch and transfer infections to patients, the wearing of face-coverings in situations like passport control or the teaching of small children where the full face needs to be visible, or the wearing of religious symbols that are also weapons, like the Sikh kirpan, in secure areas: limitations on all these seem legitimate to most people.

Disagreement comes when some suggest that public order and the protection of the rights of others should include the right not to be subjected to ostentatious religious displays in public places. They may argue that abnormally pious clothing or jewellery is in itself offensive to public sentiment in a diverse democracy. Much more seriously, they may argue that these displays seek to engender a social conformity among the religious that vulnerable people may find difficult to resist. Women may end up with their freedom of choice as compromised as that of their sisters in Saudi Arabia or Iran, even though it is peer pressure rather than the religious police depriving them of that freedom. So the argument of some secularists runs. In the Netherlands it has inspired some politicians to call for French-style secularism, because traditional toleration is no longer protecting the vulnerable. In the UK it has become case law through the case of *R (Begum) v Headteacher and Governors of Denbigh High School*, which was decided in 2006 on these grounds. Ms Begum wanted to go to school wearing a form of religious dress that covered everything apart from her face and hands. The school governors, who already allowed a form of Islamic dress agreed with parents and local religious organizations as part of its uniform, refused her request. They argued that Ms Begum had come under the influence of her extremist brother and that to grant her wish would put pressure on other girls to adopt the dress associated with such extreme understandings of Islam. The Supreme Court of the UK agreed that, specifically to avoid this possibility, Ms Begum's freedom could be limited in school.

The second challenge to secularism posed by bans like those in France is somewhat different. We saw in Chapter 5, pp. 82–6, that liberal critics of secularism make their case against it on grounds that it is unfairly discriminatory. Some of the events in France since 1989 may support their argument. It is true that the court overturned the burkini bans on secularist grounds, but many supporters of the bans also cited secularism as motive. Much of the rhetoric around the bans, of course, hinted at other less egalitarian motivations. The right-wing mayor of Villeneuve-Loubet, Lionnel Luca, said that the overturning of the ban was a boost to the 'rampant Islamisation … progressing in our country'. Anti-Muslim sentiment, stoked by shocking and extremely violent terrorist attacks by Muslims in Paris, Nice, and elsewhere in France in the preceding months undoubtedly increased support for the bans, which one opinion poll showed were favoured by over 60 per cent of French people. Certainly, right-wingers have attempted to weaponize secularism against Muslims in France, and even when not politically motivated, its insistence on dress codes undoubtedly bears down more on Muslims, Sikhs, and Jews than on Christians or atheists.

When is it right to limit freedom of religion or belief to protect others? Has secularism, allegedly neutral, become a way to oppress and exclude new minorities? Can or should it bend to accommodate minority religious believers with quite different views from the majority religion that secularism has grown up with? These questions are asked not just in relation to the wearing of religious symbols but increasingly in a much wider set of circumstances.

Religious expression in a secular state: conscience

In 1879 a US Mormon named George Reynolds, convicted for the crime of bigamy, claimed the conviction was an infringement of his constitutional rights. He argued that, because his religion made marrying multiple women a religious duty, he was protected in his bigamy by the free exercise clause and should not have been found guilty. He lost his case because the court drew a distinction between religion and the deeds motivated by religion and found that the free exercise clause protected the former but not necessarily the latter. The alternative, the court feared, would be to endorse a slippery slope which would 'make the professed doctrines of religious belief superior to the law of the land, and in effect to permit every citizen to become a law unto himself'. Opponents of the ruling could legitimately claim that this might be so, but that the law on marriage being upheld, though ostensibly secular, was in reality a Protestant Christian conception of marriage. The extent to which secular law conceals religious assumptions has been a persistent question ever since.

The question also persists whether a general law that incidentally restricts freedom of conscience for some is still in accordance with secularism. On the one hand, secularism seeks to remove domination of public life by religious dogma and religious institutions. On the other hand, it seeks to maximize the freedom of conscience of the individual within the limits of public order and the rights of others. There are times when these two aspirations clash. Granting conscientious exemptions from general laws is defended as a way of respecting freedom of religion or belief and hence of being secular. However, it can also be seen as anti-secular in that it allows a person's religion to confer benefits on them not available to their fellow citizen and, if that person is a public servant, it can be seen as an incipient or threatened domination of the public sphere by religious rules. In some countries in Europe where medical practitioners have been allowed to opt out of performing abortions on grounds of conscience, for example, the ability of women to access this service in practice can become limited. The European Committee for Social Rights upheld a complaint against Italy in 2012 on exactly these grounds.

A few cases in the UK in the early years of this century illustrated the issues some see as at stake. Individual Christians backed by Christian lobby groups sought to claim that the secular law was violating their freedom of conscience in the course of their public duties. In *Ladele v Borough of Islington*, a state registrar claimed the right to refuse to register the civil partnerships of same-sex couples; in *McFarlane v Relate Avon*, a relationship counsellor claimed the right to refuse to counsel same-sex couples; in *Chaplin v Royal Devon & Exeter Hospital*, a nurse claimed the right to wear a cross on a chain, although patient safety rules banned jewellery hanging from the neck. The cases were all lost and the religious expression of the claimants was thus limited to protect the rights of same-sex couples and of patients. This was a defeat for the claimants but a publicity victory for the lobby groups, who could add these examples of judicial oppression to their wider narrative that Christians were being persecuted by secular law. In the US, such groups have been more successful, with the Supreme Court in the case of *Burwell v Hobby Lobby* in 2014 finding that a commercial employer with a religious ethos could deny healthcare to its employees from providers that gave access to medical procedures that were against its religion.

How is the line to be drawn in cases where the two secular principles of freedom of conscience and freedom of the state from religious domination are in conflict? Is it even possible to have a general answer away from the facts of specific cases? Does a secular presumption disguise religious assumptions? Or is this claim itself the Trojan Horse of religious lobby groups attempting to de-secularize states and impose their own values?

Religious diversity in the West

Nations with non-secular constitutions can try to justify them today by saying that they simply reflect the religion or belief identity of the majority of their population. Some may even be correct in their premise: most Danes are 'Christians' and most

Chinese are 'atheists'. But in all places, society is diversifying. This is most obvious in Western countries, whose relative wealth, stability, and higher quality of life is attractive to migrants from other global regions. Migration has been a spur to secularism, especially in its aspect as equal treatment of people with different beliefs. But, ironically, secular states have also found themselves uniquely challenged by the growing diversity of their societies.

Secularism depends to some extent on citizens feeling they have a shared identity as citizens. Migration is a challenge to this solidarity in many Western societies. Our more interconnected world offers opportunities for some to adopt cosmopolitan identities that fit well with secular states. But it also means that, when people move from one country to another for economic or social reasons, they no longer need to integrate as they once did. They often find themselves in the same locality as many others from their own country of origin, and they are able, through modern media, to remain connected to their native country in spite of their physical distance. Through these means, even the children and grandchildren of migrants can feel connected to a country in which they never lived. As a result they continue to be affected by the cultural life of regions where religion in particular holds considerable sway. They may even lean harder on such cultural and transnational identities to offset the rootlessness they experience in other aspects of their lives and in their immediate social environment.

Is it the presence of such migrants and their descendants with previously unknown religions in Europe and the West that is reactivating old debates that secularism cannot contain? French secularism has only reacquired its prominence now that Muslims are a significant feature of French life. Most French associate the headscarf with Islamic extremism, especially because *l'affaire du foulard* occurred at the same time as the fatwa against Salman Rushdie. They experience the wearing of it by others as an ostentatious display of religious fundamentalism. From the point of view of some Muslim citizens, however, a commitment to a Republican civil norm is being demanded of them that is not being demanded of Catholic citizens, who can still wear crosses at will. Formal secularism and the secular political ethic of liberal democracies did develop at times when societies were more culturally homogeneous. Are they challenged by a multi-ethnic society of diverse cultures?

A second question is raised by the new presence of citizens seemingly more committed to religion than previous generations. Is secularism still democratic in a society where there are people more seriously committed to religion than before? Well, as we know by now, it depends which secularism we are talking about, but this question has certainly injected new life into an old debate. The German sociologist Jürgen Habermas used to hold firmly with John Rawls that no direct appeals to transcendent ideas could be admitted within public debate. In his more recent work, he has shifted slightly, and although he still holds that the state should have no official religion, he calls on it to recognize religion's importance. The state should be aware and appreciative of public expressions of religion because they add important dimensions to the common life of a plural society, offering identity and meaning to citizens.

The American sociologist Craig Calhoun argues that an insistence that citizens with religious belief must translate their arguments into the universally accessible language of public reason is unfair in particular to Muslims in the West. He believes that secularism as a political ethic characterizes even those Western states that have a religious establishment and that therefore this sort of injustice is endemic in liberal democratic countries. Calhoun denies that religious arguments in politics are a source of division, arguing instead that religion is what can connect citizens to each other. Like Tariq Modood, he argues religions have contributions to make to democratic life and politics and that keeping them out of politics excludes religious people and fuels less public and less reasoned sorts of resistance against politics than those that might be developed if religious people felt their religion was respected and included in the public realm.

Calhoun is surely wrong to reduce religious citizens to simply their religion. He says religion informs 'all of a believer's life', which means it's unfair to ask believers to sort out the properly political from their other beliefs, even if it's possible. But is this really true? Believers are no less human than the non-religious and surely have a wide range of reasons for their views. In addition, many religious people do subscribe to secularism, as we have seen on numerous occasions.

More generally, what would admitting religious reasons for public decisions mean in practice? That 51 per cent of the population could criminalize abortion or compel Christian prayer or impose sharia by law on the rest of society? Having a religious motivation for engaging is not the same as demanding that a religious rationale form the basis of a general law, and the former is not denied by secularism.

Is secularism too associated with the non-religious to have the objectivity it needs when confronted with the increasing diversity of today's West? There are obvious problems in this line of attack. Secularism does not require that citizens be non-religious. A secular state can coexist with a religious citizenry. A secular state can easily coexist with active religious organizations within society as NGOs, providing services and lobbying governments. It can even coexist with religious political parties, as long as those religious parties accept the secular framework for their participation. So, there is no immediately obvious reason why secularism as a political settlement is challenged by increased religiosity on the part of some citizens.

Indeed, it's far from obvious that a loosening of secularism is the answer to increasing religious diversity. On the contrary, it could equally be an incentive to strengthen secularism, perhaps moving European states that are only implicitly secular more towards the US model of becoming officially so and positively celebrating this civic value. A vivid example of this comes from the emerging secular state of Scotland. In *Belief in Dialogue* (2011), a document produced for the Scottish government by a multifaith group consulting with Muslims, Jews, Christians, and many others and chaired by a Roman Catholic nun, we read:

> Secularism…is about creating a society of equals regardless of the beliefs of those within it. Laws created in Scotland, and by the Westminster and European Parliaments, support this by seeking to eliminate discrimination and protect the rights of individuals to express and practise their beliefs. Most religious movements accept and support a secular, democratic society which allows them the freedom to practise their religious beliefs openly and without fear or recrimination from the state or any organisation, such as the police, working on behalf of the state…religious organisations are no different from other lobbying groups and it is the job of government to balance the needs and wishes of all members of society when taking decisions. The idea of a secular society is important and central to protecting equality and human rights and allowing every individual, regardless of background, to fulfil their potential as individuals and active citizens.

Still, religious diversity in the West is certainly challenging secularism in the short term. In addition to everything else, the attention paid to newer religions is in turn leading to an inflaming of sensitivity among adherents of other longer-established religions and their resurgence as political forces. Growing prominence of discussions around Islam can be linked to the rise of political Christians' demands, some of which are pre-existing, some of which are fuelled by their unwillingness to continue a self-denying privatization of their religion when they see others not doing so and not expected to do so. It is an interesting question whether some of the cases of so-called Christian persecution in the UK would have been brought if the example of politicized Islam had not gone before. The right-wing UK newspaper *The Daily Mail* carried the story of Nadia Eweida, who wished to wear a visible cross in spite of the uniform policy of her employer British Airways, under the headline, 'BA suspends a Christian for wearing a cross—but lets Muslims wear hijabs.' All over the West, a new cultural insistence on the importance of Christianity—whether religious or secularized—is being stimulated by the growing prominence of Muslims and Islam. Can secularism hold the line in the face of these trends?

In the Canadian province of Quebec, Charles Taylor was commissioned together with the academic Gérard Bouchard to make recommendations for the future of integration. In their report of 2008, they endorsed the separation of the state from any one religion but also a policy of 'reasonable accommodation', which would allow accommodations to religious requirements as long as they did not compromise other fundamental values like gender equality. Religious holidays in addition to the Christian ones could become legitimate causes for employment leave, and school pupils who wished to would be able to wear religious symbols in public schools. There is an obvious resonance of this principle with the 'equal treatment' aspect of secularism. Might that fact recommend some variant of it to secular states in the future as the way of dealing with the emerging hyper-diversity of Western societies and defusing the resulting tensions?

Resurgent political religion

The oldest challenge to secularism is political religion, and this is far from a spent force. After a 20th century in which it seemed to diminish, the early 21st century offers evidence of its resurgence. We see transnational religious NGOs of every type lobbying intensively in states and international institutions on a global scale that recalls the overweening ambition of the Roman Catholic Church in pre-modern Europe. They fight to roll back secularism in national laws and constitutions and to impose their values on society and the state. In political culture, we see Christian ethnic nationalism in Europe and the US, Hindu nationalism in India and amongst the Indian diaspora, and Islamic extremism in the Arab world and globally. In some states it poses a possibly fatal challenge to secularism.

We saw in Chapter 5 how romantic conservatism in India gave rise to the concept of *Hindutva* in the 1920s. *Hindutva* has gone on to be adopted as the official ideology of the conservative Indian People's Party (BJP). Founded in 1980, the party grew rapidly at a local and regional level and won the national general election in 2014. Its official website, while declaring pride in Hindus' history of 'tolerance for other faiths and respect for diversity of spiritual experiences', dwells chillingly on the 'cold-blooded slaughter' perpetrated by the Muslim invaders of history and claims that Hindus in modern times have been oppressed in their own country by a 'pseudo-secularism' which has given too much away to followers of 'other' religions: an unequal compromise by Hinduism with alien creeds. Ministers in the BJP government of Prime Minister Narendra Modi have spoken of the need to 'cleanse' Indian culture of foreign religions like Islam and Christianity, and other BJP politicians have advocated the adoption of the Hindu sacred text *Bhagavad Gita* as the official 'national scripture'. Communal violence against Muslims and violent assaults, even murders, of those alleged to have violated Hindu religious norms by eating beef have gone unpunished (see Figure 7). An attempt to have BJP candidates banned for this political use of religion, which is unlawful in India, as we saw in Chapter 3, pp. 43–4, has foundered on courts' rulings that *Hindutva* is not a religion. Well-grounded fears that the BJP would like to do away with secularism in the constitution persist.

We saw in Chapter 3 how *laiklik* in Turkey was from the start an elite project and how the vast majority of the population remained unattached to its principles. The conservative Justice and

7. Family of Muslim Mohammad Akhlaq, lynched with impunity by a Hindu mob in India for allegedly killing a cow in 2015.

Development Party (AKP) is the latest political movement to capitalize on this popular discontent. Founded in 2001, it won the general election of 2002 and has governed Turkey ever since. The party's roots lie in the frankly Islamist parties of the late 20th century, but its leader and the current president of Turkey, Recep Tayyip Erdogan, has denied to foreign critics that it is an Islamist party, claiming it is only politically and socially conservative. In the context of Turkish history, it is easy to see why the AKP would want to avoid these connotations: legal efforts to ban the AKP for the political use of religion failed in court by the vote of only one judge. Its supporters, however, come from the devout sections of Turkish society, no longer just rural peasants, but their urbanized and entrepreneurial descendants in the town. Like the BJP, the AKP appeals to and represents economic modernity as well as religious conservatism. In government, the party has chipped away at secularism. It has overturned bans on headscarves in a number of public establishments (see Figure 8). The Religious Affairs Directorate has turned from a state

8. Turkish secularists in 2008 protesting against Erdogan's proposal to allow the headscarf at universities.

department controlling religion to an effective establishment of Hanafi Sunni Islam, issuing fatwas as well as administering the only denomination favoured with state funding.

The year 2016 saw an escalation of this anti-secularist tendency. The Speaker of the Turkish Parliament, Ismail Kahraman, charged with drafting a new constitution, said it was wrong that God was not mentioned in the current one and that 'We are a Muslim country and so we should have a religious constitution...Secularism would not have a place in a new constitution.' The call to prayer was chanted from the ancient mosque and former church of Hagia Sophia for the first time since it was turned into a museum by the government of Atatürk. Most significantly, a large-scale crackdown in the wake of a failed coup has intensified the persecution of minorities, dissenters, and political secularists, who have been censored, removed from their jobs, arrested, imprisoned, or tortured in their tens of thousands. *Yeni Şafak*, a newspaper supportive of the government (most unsupportive newspapers have either been closed or had their staff arrested), which frequently publishes anti-Semitic material, ended the year with the headline 'Secularism enslaved the Middle East, Islam will free it once again'. The fast moving pace of current Turkish politics may yet see secularism eliminated formally from the constitution as well as from reality.

These religiously inclined political parties are mass movements: the AKP has ten million members; the BJP has 110 million. But rising political religion is a challenge not just for democratic republics. Non-democratic secular regimes in the Arab world, like that of President Assad in Syria, are similarly under pressure from resurgent religious movements, just like those which overturned more secular regimes in Iran and Afghanistan in the 20th century. The idea of secularism as progress has lost ground in the Arab world, where conservative Islam along Saudi Arabian lines is now seen as the dominant alternative to established political orders.

Christian organizations are just as active. The biggest transnational NGOs seeking to subvert secularism are evangelical Protestant ones, funded out of the US to operate in Europe, Asia, and Africa. The Roman Catholic Church, recognized as a state in many international institutions like the UN, increasingly seeks to impose its doctrine through international treaties ('concordats') with states. In the US many right-wing Republicans including those around President Donald Trump carry on the American anti-secularist tradition that wants to see Christianity in the constitution. Steve Bannon, who went on to be the president's chief strategist, in an address broadcast to a right-wing religious conference at the Vatican in 2014, called for politics in the West to reconnect with its 'Judaeo-Christian' roots and values. Since coming to office, Trump's administration has pursued religiously motivated policies that subvert the secular nature of the American constitution and seems to stand ready to support the same attitude globally.

When these various religio-political movements combine with each other at the international level and with non-secular regimes of different types such as Russia, China, or the Muslim-majority states of Southeast Asia—as they increasingly do—they can threaten secular settlements worldwide.

In other parts of the world, secular constitutions are not enforced. Sometimes the state is not powerful enough to do so, as in Nigeria, whose constitution prohibits the establishment of any religion nationally or within the constituent states, but where a number of states have adopted sharia as state law in spite of this prohibition and with impunity. In many places there is a lack of institutions to check government, or governments may not wish to enforce secular provisions, either because they disagree with them or because they have another interest that is more important to them.

Secularism challenged as never before?

Secularism had its challenges even in its global heyday, when political elites paid lip service to freedom of religion or belief in principle but not often in practice. Nonetheless, the cessation even of lip service to secularism, the replacement of early 20th-century secular states in the Arab world in particular with Islamic states, the increase in discrimination and mixing up of religion and the state that is occurring in so many nations, the rise of ethnic nationalism and totalitarian politics all over the globe, and the increasing rejection of democracy and liberalism—these all combine to threaten secularism as never before.

Greater numbers of people are claiming religious identities globally every year. Many who barely practise a religion and have no personal religious beliefs increasingly claim them as a cultural self-identity. In Western states, this raises democratic and human rights questions for secularism that, especially when posed on its own political terms of freedom and equality, offer a complex challenge. The risk is that secularists—especially Western liberal ones, who already often feel a sort of guilt at the past treatment of African and Asian societies by their nation states—develop a certain insecurity in light of this. Such a loss of self-confidence will further dilute secularism's appeal and obscure the positive transformative effect that secularism has had and can have on human freedom, equality, and peace.

Afterword: the future
of secularism

Secularism is like every political agenda in that it can be realized in either a liberal or a draconian way. It can be introduced democratically, with public consent, subject to the rule of law, carefully implemented in a way that seeks to respect the human rights of those of all beliefs. It can also, especially when seen simply as separation of state and religion, be imposed by violence, accompanied by the persecution of its opponents, designed to exclude dissenters and homogenize society, enforced by totalitarian regulation. This fact is nothing to do with secularism as such. These are the two means by which any political settlement, whether socialism, nationalism, even democracy, has always been initiated. They should not distract us from the essential nature of secularism itself.

A world in which all people believed the same things and had the same culture would be a dull one. It would deprive us all of the enormous benefit that the interaction of different perspectives has for intellectual progress. It would deprive our individual lives of many of the experiences that give them colour and depth. Such a world is also profoundly unlikely. When free, people make choices that differ from those made by others. As soon as even two people's choices on big questions differ, society becomes eternally diverse. Still, however different we may be from one another, we are also gregarious and have more in common at the level of our social needs than divides us. Even in a world of diversity, we need a framework for our common life and most of us want that framework to be a fair one.

On balance, some version of the principle of secularism offers this possibility. Certainly it is imperfect—no political settlement is perfect. But it is the only plausible principle on offer. Perhaps it is impossible to attain completely—societies evolve and no system is forever. But that does not mean that moving ever closer towards it is not better than the alternative. Secularism as a dynamic and ongoing process of negotiation between equals seems to me to be the best way of organizing our common life in a way that is fair to all in the context of diversity. If we do not attempt progress towards it, especially at a time of heightened global tensions and confrontations, the future may be as grim as the days of the wars of religion that first made secularism so necessary.

References and further reading

Chapter 1: What is secularism?

George Jacob Holyoake recounts his own coining of 'secularism' in *Principles of Secularism Illustrated* (1871). Jean Baubérot has published widely on secularism and any of his work in the last ten years illustrates his definition. He also has a blog at https://blogs.mediapart.fr/jean-bauberot/blog (accessed 2 Mar. 2017). The Human Rights Committee's 1993 words are in its General Comment 22, online at http://hrlibrary.umn.edu/gencomm/hrcom22.htm (accessed 2 Mar. 2017). Quotes from Alan Carling are from the first chapter of his *The Social Equality of Religion or Belief* (Palgrave Macmillan, 2016).

Chapter 2: Secularism in Western societies

The Oxford World's Classics series provides good modern translations of both Aristotle's *Politics* (2009) and *Selected Philosophical Writings* of Aquinas (2008). The full text of Locke's *A Letter Concerning Toleration* is available at http://www.constitution.org/jl/tolerati.htm (accessed 2 Mar. 2017), Montesquieu's *The Spirit of the Laws* at http://www.constitution.org/cm/sol.htm (accessed 2 Mar. 2017), Rousseau's *Of the Social Contract* at http://www.earlymoderntexts.com/assets/pdfs/rousseau1762.pdf (accessed 2 Mar. 2017), d'Holbach's *Christianity Unveiled* at http://www.ftarchives.net/holbach/unveiled/cucontents.htm (accessed 2 Mar. 2017). Jefferson's letter to the Danbury Baptists is online at http://www.constitution.org/tj/sep_church_state.htm (accessed 2 Mar. 2017). President Reagan gave his speech at Temple Hillel in Valley Stream, NY, on 26 October 1984 and the video is online at https://www.youtube.com/watch?v=rfgxbGvW-7E (accessed 2 Mar. 2017).

The constitution.org website provides a number of key legal texts instrumental in the development of liberal secular norms in the West. Introductions to a number of the historical movements and events referred to in this chapter can be found in the OUP Very Short Introduction series, including *Christianity* by Linda Woodhead (2004), *The Enlightenment* by John Robertson (2015), *The French Revolution* by William Doyle (2001), *The Founding Fathers* by R. B. Bernstein (2015), and *The American Revolution* by Robert J. Allison (2015). A good recent re-examination of secularism in ancient Europe is Tim Whitmarsh's *Battling the Gods: Atheism in the Ancient World* (Faber and Faber, 2016). The best recent account of the Reformation is Diarmaid MacCulloch's *Reformation: Europe's House Divided 1490–1700* (Penguin, 2004).

Chapter 3: Secularism diversifies

Quotes from Ataturk can be found at http://www.columbia.edu/~sss31/Turkiye/ata/hayati.html#trans (accessed 2 Mar. 2017). The constitutions of Turkey and India—and of all the states mentioned in Chapter 6—can be found at https://www.constituteproject.org (accessed 2 Mar. 2017). Quotes from Gandhi here and in Chapter 4 can be found at http://www.thehindu.com/2003/10/22/stories/2003102200891000.htm (accessed 2 Mar. 2017).

A good exploration of the secularisms across this chapter and Chapter 2 is found in Ahmet Kuru's *Secularism and State Policy toward Religion: The United States, France and Turkey* (Cambridge University Press, 2007). The pace of events in Turkey means standard works are dating rapidly, but Hakan Yavuz's *Secularism and Muslim Democracy in Turkey* (Cambridge University Press, 2009) is essential. *Secularism and its Critics*, edited by Rajeev Bhargava (Oxford University Press, 1999), contains further reflections on Indian secularism. More generally on Asia, both *The Future of Secularism*, edited by T. N. Srinivasan (Oxford University Press, 2007) and *Varieties of Secularism in Asia: Anthropological Explorations of Religion, Politics and the Spiritual*, edited by Nils Ole Bubandt and

Martijn Van Beek (Routledge, 2012) offer further reading. Ranging more widely than secularism, Peter van der Veer's *The Modern Spirit of Asia* (Princeton University Press, 2014) is a fascinating introduction to spirituality and modernity in China and India. Elizabeth Shakman Hurd's *The Politics of Secularism in International Relations* (Princeton University Press, 2008) is vital further reading on the international dimension.

Chapter 4: The case for secularism

J. S. Mill's *On Liberty* (1859) is available at http://www.bartleby.com/130/ (accessed 2 Mar. 2017). *The Baptist Faith and Message* is at http://www.sbc.net/bfm2000/bfm2000.asp (accessed 2 Mar. 2017). John Rawls's *A Theory of Justice* (1971) is published by the Harvard University Press. The *Suttapitaka* are available in a number of translations including *Sayings of the Buddha*, translated by Rupert Gethin (Oxford University Press, 2008). The two stories from the Christian Bible are from the Book of Mark and the Book of John respectively.

The Case for Secularism: A Neutral State in an Open Society, edited by Richard Norman (British Humanist Association, 2014) is a short rehearsal of arguments for secularism by liberal philosophers and Paul Cliteur's *The Secular Outlook: In Defense of Moral and Political Secularism* (Wiley-Blackwell, 2010) argues the case at greater length.

Chapter 5: The case against secularism

Khomeini's *Islamic Government* is at http://www.iranchamber.com/history/rkhomeini/books/velayat_faqeeh.pdf (accessed 2 Mar. 2017). Bishop Nazir Ali's remarks are from his interview on *Today* on BBC Radio 4, 6 November 2006. Queen Elizabeth II's speech is online at https://www.royal.uk/queens-speech-lambeth-palace-15-february-2012 (accessed 2 Mar. 2017). Burke's *Reflections on the Revolution in France* is online at http://www.constitution.org/eb/rev_fran.htm (accessed 2 Mar. 2017). Sarkozy's 2007 speech is at http://www.lemonde.fr/politique/article/2007/12/21/discours-du-president-de-la-republique-dans-la-salle-de-la-signature-du-palais-du-latran_992170_823448.html (accessed 2 Mar. 2017) and his 2008 speech at http://www.lemonde.fr/politique/ article/2008/04/24/discours-de-nicolas-sarkozy-a-riyad-le-14-janvier-2008_1038207_823448.html (accessed 2 Mar. 2017). Sarvakar's comments on *Hindutva* can be found at *Hindu Nationalism: A Reader*, edited by Christophe Jaffrelot (Princeton University Press, 2007), p. 94.

A range of interesting perspectives on the UK situation is provided by *Church and State in 21st Century Britain: The Future of Church Establishment*, edited by R. M. Morris (Palgrave, 2009). A political theorist's full broadside against secularism can be found in William E. Connolly's *Why I Am Not a Secularist* (University of Minnesota Press, 1999). Talal Asad's *Formations of the Secular: Christianity, Islam, Modernity* (Stanford University Press, 2003) is also essential reading in this vein. Most modern non-theocratic critics of secularism, however, position themselves as wanting to modify or reformulate it and their works are best considered under Chapter 6 of this book.

Chapter 6: Conceptions of secularism

The quote from Jose Casanova is from his excellent 'The Secular, Secularizations, Secularism', in *Rethinking Secularism* (Oxford University Press, 2011), edited by Craig Calhoun, Mark Juergensmeyer, and Jonathan Vanantwerpen. Charles Taylor's magisterial *A Secular Age* (Harvard University Press, 2007) expresses the thought attributed to him here and many others. Elizabeth Shakman Hurd elaborates on her two types in 'Varieties of Secularism', in *The Politics of Secularism in International Relations* (Princeton University Press, 2008) pp. 23–45, as well as elsewhere. The broad definition of secularism by Modood is from his 2011 Paul Hanly Furfey lecture. The first two quotes from Stepan are from his 'The Multiple Secularisms of Modern Democratic and Non-Democratic Regimes', in *Rethinking Secularism*. The third is from http://blogs.ssrc.org/ tif/2012/06/15/twin-tolerations-today-an-interview-with-alfred-stepan/ (accessed 2 Mar. 2017). Bhargava's first quote here is from his 'Parekh's Multiculturalism and Secularism: Religions in Public Life', in *Multiculturalism Rethought*, edited by Varun Uberoi and Tariq Modood (Edinburgh University Press, 2015); the second is from his 'Political Secularism', in *The Oxford Handbook of Political Theory*, edited by Anne Phillips, Bonnie Honig, and John Dryzek (Oxford University Press, 2006). Rowan Williams elaborated his distinction in *Secularism, Faith and Freedom*, a lecture given at the Vatican on 23 November 2006. Quotes from Modood under 'Proliferating

Secularisms' are from his working paper for the European University Institute at http://cadmus.eui.eu/bitstream/handle/1814/36484/RSCAS_2015_47.pdf?sequence=1&isAllowed=y (accessed 2 Mar. 2017). The website of British Muslims for Secular Democracy is bmsd.org.uk, of the National Secular Society, secularism.org.uk, and of Humanists UK (formerly the British Humanist Association), humanists.uk.

Rethinking Secularism, referred to earlier, and *Comparative Secularisms in a Global Age*, edited by Linell E. Cady and Elizabeth Shakman Hurd (Palgrave, 2010), are essential reading for those wanting to read in greater depth a range of possible reconceptualizations of secularism today. Just as wide-ranging and thought-provoking are *Religion, Secularism, and Constitutional Democracy*, edited by Jean L. Cohen and Cécile Laborde (Columbia University Press, 2016), *Constitutional Secularism in an Age of Religious Revival*, edited by Susanna Mancini and Michel Rosenfeld (Oxford University Press, 2014), and *The Social Equality of Religion or Belief*, edited by Alan Carling (Palgrave, 2016). These three volumes are multidisciplinary approaches and also contain further reading relevant to Chapter 7 of this book.

Chapter 7: Hard questions and new conflicts

Jonathan Fox's latest published analysis of his data is in his *Political Secularism, Religion, and the State* (Cambridge University Press, 2015). The *Jyllands-Posten* editorial is quoted in an article on the affair by Kenan Malik at https://www.indexoncensorship.org/2012/12/enemies-of-free-speech/ (accessed 2 Mar. 2017) and Malik's book *From Fatwa to Jihad: The Rushdie Affair and Its Legacy* (Atlantic Books, 2017) is excellent further reading. A good recent article on Hindu campaigns for censorship in the West is http://www.latimes.com/nation/la-na-hindu-products-commercial-inappropriate-20161221-story.html (accessed 2 Mar. 2017). Judgements of the French Council of State are all available on their website at http://www.conseil-etat.fr/ (accessed 2 Mar. 2017). Habermas's current views are well-reflected in his 'Religion in the Public Sphere', *European Journal of Philosophy* 14/1 (2006). 1 25. The Scottish report *Belief in Dialogue* is at http://www.interfaithscotland.org/resources/publications/belief-in-dialogue/ (accessed 2 Mar. 2017). The report of the Bouchard and Taylor Commission was published as *Building the Future: A Time for*

Reconciliation, Abridged Report (2008) by the Government of Quebec. The *Daily Mail* headline on Eweida appeared above the print version of the story at http://www.dailymail.co.uk/news/article-412609/ Fury-BA-says-allow-Muslim-veil-cross.html (accessed 2 Mar. 2017). References to the BJP website in this chapter are all to the page http://www.bjp.org/index.php?option=com_content&view=article&id =369:hindutva-the-great-nationalist-ideology&Itemid=501 (accessed 2 Mar. 2017). Ismail Kahraman is quoted at http://www.telegraph.co. uk/news/2016/04/25/turkeys-parliament-speaker-seeks-religious-constitution/ (accessed 2 Mar. 2017). The *Yeni Şafak* headline can be found at http://www.yenisafak.com/en/columns/yusufkaplan/ secularism-enslaved-the-middle-east-islam-will-free-it-once-again-2033795 (accessed 2 Mar. 2017).

Good journalism from a number of outlets provides increasing coverage of the issues discussed in this chapter, which in the cases of the US, France, India, and Turkey are all fast-moving. All the multi-contributor works referred to under every preceding chapter address themes in this chapter and the following highlighted works also offer further reading:

An-na'im, A. A. *Islam and the Secular State: Negotiating the Future of Shari'a* (Harvard University Press, 2008).

Bradney, A. *Law and Faith in a Sceptical Age* (Routledge, 2009).

Davies, Lynn. *Unsafe Gods: Security, Secularism and Schooling* (Institute of Education Press, 2014).

Elver, Hilal. *The Headscarf Controversy: Secularism and Freedom of Religion* (Oxford University Press, 2012).

Fetzer, J. S. and Soper, J. C. *Muslims and the State in Britain, France and Germany* (Cambridge University Press, 2009).

Haworth, Alan (ed.). *Right to Object? Conscientious Objection and Religious Conviction* (British Humanist Association, 2011).

Levey, G. B. and Modood, Tariq. *Secularism, Religion and Multicultural Citizenship* (Cambridge University Press, 2008).

MacLure, J. and Taylor, C. *Secularism and Freedom of Conscience* (Harvard University Press, 2011).

Tamimi, Azzam and Esposito, John L. *Islam and Secularism in the Middle East* (New York University Press, 2000).

Warner, Michael, Vanantwerpen, Jonathan, and Calhoun, Craig (eds.). *Varieties of Secularism in a Secular Age* (Harvard University Press, 2010).

Index

SOCIAL MEDIA
Very Short Introduction

Join our community

www.oup.com/vsi

- Join us online at the official Very Short Introductions
  Facebook page.
- Access the thoughts and musings of our authors with our
  online **blog**.
- Sign up for our monthly **e-newsletter** to receive information
  on all new titles publishing that month.
- Browse the full range of Very Short Introductions online.
- Read **extracts** from the Introductions for free.
- If you are a teacher or lecturer you can order inspection
  copies quickly and simply via our website.